How to Network in College

in College

A practical guide to student success in the networking age

Isaac V. Serwanga

ISBN-13: 978-1539714118
ISBN-10: 153971411X

DEDICATION

To you, the college student.

"The only person you are destined to be, is the person you decide to be."

Ralph Waldo Emerson

CONTENTS

ACKNOWLEDGMENTS..vii

PREFACE ix

INTRODUCTION xv

SECTION I: THE FOUNDATION.................................xxi

1 WHAT IS NETWORKING? 1

2 NETWORKING STARTS WITH YOU........................... 13

3 OWN YOUR PERSONAL BRAND............................... 27

SECTION II: THE TOOLS 43

4 THE NETWORKING E-MAIL 45

5 THE ART OF NETWORKING 61

6 THINK BIG(GER) 91

SECTION III: THE OUTREACH 103

7 ON-CAMPUS NETWORKING...................................105

8 OFF-CAMPUS NETWORKING..................................123

9 THE POWER OF MENTORSHIP 133

10 TIME MANAGEMENT: 10 TIPS FOR SUCCESS............145

CONCLUSION...163

ABOUT THE AUTHOR..167

ACKNOWLEDGMENTS

A special thank you to each and every one of the young men of the Profound Ivy mentorship program. This book is not possible without your trust, commitment, and execution. Well done, fellas.

PREFACE

How this book will help you

The best way I can think of to describe how this book will help you is to tell you about how it would have helped *me* when I was a college student.

If I had the chance to do college all over again, I would step onto the campus of Princeton University feeling more prepared than ever after reading this book and mapping out the steps to my future. I'd use the book's simple strategies to develop long-lasting relationships with my professors, to cultivate new friendships beyond my social comfort zone, to find and land the perfect job, and to build a professional network that would extend well beyond the confines of campus. I'd revisit these pages many times to find both the information and the inspiration necessary to go after my loftiest goals with the utmost confidence.

If I had the chance to do college over again, I'd challenge myself to grow both personally and professionally by applying the concepts presented in these pages. I would know that the foundation of *any* kind of success is a deep understanding of who I am. I would enthusiastically take the time to discover my passions, strengths, and interests. I would build my own personal brand around my distinct personal qualities; I would build my professional network around my personal brand; and I would draw upon this amazing network to build my life. I'd be reassured in knowing that by proceeding in this structured, meticulous way, I wouldn't have to chase after opportunities; instead, opportunities would chase after me. If I could do college all over again, I'd use this book as my guide to ensure that I'd get every cent—and then some—out of my $200,000 investment.

This book is a roadmap for success in college. All of the ways that these strategies could have helped me are now available to you. My recommendation? Don't overlook anything in this book until you try it for yourself. This book and your network are no different: to reap the benefits, you've got to put the concepts to work.

Why I wrote this book

For the last two years, I have been sharing this book's ideas and concepts with some amazing students at Princeton University. When we first began, I was hard-pressed to find ten students who would show up at our meeting. In less than a year's time, more than forty students were voluntarily giving up an hour of their precious Sunday afternoons to learn about the benefits of building relationships across campus—the benefits of networking. They were seeing results, and nothing speaks louder than results. After attending one of our workshops, even the University president lauded the efforts of the Profound Ivy mentorship program. So, I wrote this book partly because I want to spread the word about ideas that have a proven track record of success.

Here's my second reason. I knew that if I could go to a prestigious university like Princeton and find myself unemployed upon graduation, it was likely that tens of thousands of graduates across the country could find themselves in a similar predicament. Networking not only landed me my desired job; it helped me turn my dire situation on its head. Through networking, I landed job offers from the NCAA, J.P. Morgan, and Princeton University—all within the same month.

Third, I wrote this book because I believe in the power of its message. Getting a job is very important to college students, and legitimately so. But the benefits of networking extend beyond the professional realm. Networking can change every aspect of your life. Learning how to build relationships sparked a transformation in my life and in the lives of the students I've mentored. Knowing how to communicate who you are effectively and how to build meaningful relationships with virtually anyone you meet will have a monumental impact on your life and on how you view your college experience. Effective networking will ensure that opportunities beat down your door, but who you become in the process is the most valuable gift of all.

How to use this book

The book is divided into three sections: "The Foundation," "The Tools," and "The Outreach." "The Foundation" will help walk you step-by-step through the several aspects of personal development prior to networking with others. Building off that foundation, "The Tools" is a compilation of practical tools that help you to reach out and network in one-on-one settings. As we walk through networking events and other situations, we'll discuss what to watch out for and how to perform at your best, whether over email or a cup of coffee. Then we wrap up with "The Outreach." This section details the benefits of both on- and off-campus relationships and provides tips, strategies, and examples of the best ways to create your personal network and to find—and become—a mentor. Last but not least, we close with bonus chapter 10 which provides you with ten proven time-management tips to help you maximize your time in college.

Feel free to read the chapters and sections in whatever order you like, and revisit sections that best apply to your situation. Come job-hunting season, you may want to visit chapter 5, "The Art of Networking," to learn more about the best way to make a first impression. If it's the holiday season and you have some time on your hands, you may want to read chapter 4, "The Networking E-mail," to learn how best to reach out to people you want to include in your network. Chapter 10, "Time Management: Ten Tips for Success," will come in handy when midterms and finals roll around and you want to get more time out of your days (and nights).

However you decide to read this book, I suggest you constantly ask yourself the following question: how can I apply what I'm reading to my current situation? Please note: At the end of each chapter you will find "Chapter Takeaways" as well as "Calls to Action." The chapter takeaways provide you with a brief summary of the main points made in the chapter. The calls to action are filled with actionable steps and exercises you can apply immediately to practice these concepts. These features are present to help reinforce the networking concepts all throughout the book. Don't just *read* the book. Make sure you set aside time to apply these practices and develop your networking skills along the way.

How to Network in College was written to help guide you to your success. This book is action oriented for a reason. Be prepared to make some changes and allow the results to speak for themselves.

INTRODUCTION

On Tuesday, June 4, 2013, I walked through FitzRandolph Gate and graduated from Princeton University. It was a day packed with overwhelming emotion and joyous celebration. I felt incredibly accomplished. With the reassuring support and love of friends and family, I had made it through some of the most demanding years of my life. For most of us, college graduation is the pinnacle of our educational career. It symbolizes all the work we do from kindergarten to commencement.

However, this state of nostalgia and accomplishment passed just as quickly as it had arrived. It wasn't but a day after the sounds of speeches subsided, the tears of joy dried up, the risers were broken down, and the homebound flights were boarded that my stomach began to churn with fear of the immediate future. For the first time in my life, the next step was not scripted. I was an unemployed college graduate without a clue of where to go or what to do. The adage was certainly true for me: there is no greater fear than fear of the unknown. And I had experienced no bigger unknown than that of life after college.

It was a harsh reality to swallow, being an unemployed Ivy League graduate. But as I began to come to terms with my situation and to speak with friends and other college graduates about theirs, I realized that by no measure was I the rare exception. This was both comforting and shocking. The reality was that my predicament as an unemployed college grad was common. College graduates all across the country were having a difficult time finding jobs. According to a study conducted by the Economic Policy Institute, the unemployment rate for workers under the age of twenty-five was twice as high as the national unemployment rate. Over a third of the nation's 2013 graduating class was working in jobs that didn't require a college degree.

What's more, many of my close friends who had jobs were scared that they had landed the *wrong* jobs. Finding a happily employed college graduate was like finding a diamond in the rough.

Disgruntled college graduates like me were one of three things: unemployed, underemployed, or misemployed. That is, they were unable to find a job, they had found a job that was well below their education level, or they had settled for a job that had nothing to do with the work they had intended to find. Why was this the case? Why were we in this predicament?

In the following months, the tide began to turn for me. My interest in athletics led me to an internship with an organization in Northern California that organized high school athletic championships. The position wasn't glitzy, to say the least, but it did provide me the opportunity to gain some experience in the athletics world, an industry I wanted to pursue. The internship was part-time, so I spent the majority of my days searching the web for jobs and applying like a madman to anything that I thought would sound good when people asked me what jobs I was applying to. I was a misguided mess, desperately looking for someone to save me rather than saving myself. I vividly remember asking myself repeatedly, "Why is this job-hunting process so difficult? What am I doing wrong?"

Then I read a book someone had given to me as a graduation present, and the lightbulb turned on for me. The book was *Never Eat Alone* by Keith Ferrazzi. It's littered with examples of how Ferrazzi discovered as a young professional that building relationships was perhaps the most integral contributor to the success he's experienced in his career. I loved the concepts as well as the brutally honest delivery. Ferrazzi's message was exactly what I needed to hear at exactly the right time. Upon finishing the book, I immediately decided to apply what I had learned to my own situation. If these concepts could work for Ferrazzi, why couldn't they work for me? I was desperate for answers and had nothing to lose.

Following Ferrazzi's advice, I changed my approach to job-hunting. Instead of looking for jobs, I began to look for people. I attended conferences and lectures that interested me. I reached out to professors and friends who hadn't heard from me in years and rekindled relationships. I also grew comfortable with being uncomfortable. For instance, I spoke with strangers in coffee shops and went out of my way to be of service to people who didn't have any obvious way to help me. I began to identify my strengths and to put them on display everywhere I went. Little did I know that I was strengthening my weak networking muscles. At first, this approach felt different, and it was more exhausting than anything I had ever done. I began to realize that I hadn't just changed my job-hunting technique; I had changed my everyday life. The results were more dramatic than anything I'd ever experienced.

Less than nine months after graduation, I had received four job offers. The first was from J.P. Morgan, one of the top banking institutions in the world. The second came from the NCAA, for a position that had attracted over 650 applicants. The third offer was from a marketing firm in New York City, with a starting salary of $70,000. The last job offer was for an athletic administrator position at Princeton, my beloved alma mater.

I couldn't have written a better script for the unfolding of events in my life at the time. While I was amazed at the results, I was more amazed at how the results had come about. The four offers I had received had one common thread: networking. I had shown people who I was. I had found a way to build the relationships necessary to prepare me for the interviews, and this action had transformed me from "an applicant" to "Isaac, the standout applicant." Sure, I had gone above and beyond to prepare for the interviews, and this preparation had contributed to my success. But had it not been for some strategic networking, I wouldn't have received any of those job offers. To go one step further, I wouldn't have known some of the organizations were even hiring if not for this beautiful concept we call networking.

I was blown away. The results I had generated sparked a fire in me, and I wanted to learn more. I wanted to share what I had learned with young people who would inevitably face the same predicament in college. I decided to accept the job offer from Princeton and to work in athletics, staying close to friends and former teammates so that I could share this incredible information. I then went on to cocreate Profound Ivy, a mentoring program that started with roughly ten students and grew to about forty students by the year's end. A former college teammate of mine and I gave lecture after lecture, impressing upon students the power of networking and the positive impact it would have on their future careers. In one of our first meetings, I asked my mentees to ponder this question: "If I could get these kinds of results in just a few months, what do you think you could do for yourself in four years?"

Profound Ivy was a success, and it still is. Right before my eyes, I saw mentees take our advice and build relationships not just for the sake of future employment opportunities but also for the sake of personal development. They were transforming their college experiences by building communities and helping each other position themselves for success in college and beyond. Over the course of the year, something unexpected also happened. I began to learn from Profound Ivy mentees just as much as they had learned from me. Over time it became clear that the highest-achieving students in our program were well known among their peers, their coaches, and many of the administrators across campus. These high achievers were actively involved in multiple groups and initiatives at Princeton. They thought outside the box and created ways to attract opportunities as opposed to chasing them.

After sharing what I had learned for two years and studying the ways in which some of my students had maximized their college experience, I wanted desperately to share these transformative ideas so that all students could benefit. I remembered the fear of the unknown that I had experienced after graduation, and I knew that networking while in college was the remedy to that fear. I took all I had learned, all that I wished I had known in college, and put it all in the book you are now reading: *How to Network in College.*

So, dive in. Don't just read this book; use it! Commit yourself to building your network because it might be the most important thing you do in college. Read these chapters to help spark your own ideas. Use this book to create the relationships you wish to have, to sculpt the environments you wish to be part of, and to seize the opportunity that lies right before your eyes. Above all, I want you to come away with the conviction that the one person who can make your college experience everything you want it to be is *you.*

SECTION I.
THE FOUNDATION

1 WHAT IS NETWORKING?

Relationships are all there is. Everything in the universe only exists because it is in relationship to everything else. Nothing exists in isolation.

—Keith Ferrazzi, *Never Eat Alone*

The Networked Age

It is far from exaggerated speech when LinkedIn cofounder and executive chairman Reid Hoffman refers to the world we live in today as *the networked age.* The exponential growth in 21st century technology has successfully shrunken the globe and has provided us with a multitude of ways to make new connections. Social media is a great example of this—we can use our platform to gain knowledge and interact with individuals we've never met, discover companies we never knew existed, and even create opportunities we never could've imagined in the past. We are now more connected than ever, and the possibilities for what we choose to pursue with our career—and our lives—are limited only by the amount of effort we choose to invest in our endeavors.

But *the networked age* is not just defined by technology. This era Hoffman refers to must rely just as much on human-to-human interaction as it does the virtual aspect of networking. We can add individual after individual to our LinkedIn network, but at some point we will have to show up in person and make those integral personal connections. In today's world, there is no doubt that the person who has fine-tuned this skillset of relationship building both in person and online has put him or herself at a distinct advantage. This individual can thrive in this networked world simply because they understand the incredible power of relationships. Hoffman puts it best. *"What really matters in the networked age? Relationships. Relationships help you find opportunities, resources, make decisions more effectively, and manage a long-term investment and a lifetime career."*

Why network in college?

College is the *perfect* time for you to begin networking for two distinct reasons: access and time.

1) College students have incredible access on a college campus.

It is not uncommon to find a college or university as the beating heart and central hub of its city. On a college campus you are bound to find a student body population with individuals from all over the country if not the world, as well as distinguished professors and polished college administrators. Additionally, each one of the 5300 American colleges and universities have proud alumni who remain involved with their school. To network effectively you need access to resources, and there is not a place with more access to the right resources, the right people and the right opportunities than a college campus.

2) College students have time on their side.

Yes, even *you* have time. College is certainly a busy, but its much more a battle of priorities than it is about time. An investment in networking is an investment in *your future*. If you don't have time for your own future, then it's time to reevaluate what it is that is taking up your time.

Networking and playing a sport are very similar in the sense that the more time you can dedicate to perfecting your craft, the better you become. If a basketball player practices perfecting his jump shot daily and another player practices weekly, who would become the better shooter after one year of practice? Of course it would be the player who practiced daily. Networking is *no different*. As a college student, you have time on your side. The freshman who reads this book and begins applying the principles of networking immediately will be better off than if he or she waited a few years to begin. Networking has a compound effect—the longer you invest, the greater the results. While in college, you can make networking a part of your college experience and use these fundamental years in your life to build the relationships necessary for both your personal and professional growth.

So, what is networking?

Networking is the process of cultivating goal-oriented, mutualistic relationships for the purpose of personal or professional development. The type of networking we'll be discussing in this book is called goal-oriented networking. Sometimes your networking goal will be direct and obvious—a job opportunity, a referral to someone else, words of advice, or exposure to someone with similar or dissimilar interests. Other times, the benefit of a new relationship will be indirect; it will come into play in ways you couldn't possibly have imagined. Either way, it's important to start with the idea that the relationships you actively develop have the potential to lead you closer to a goal you've identified.

Delving Deeper

So, beyond the brief definition above, what *is* networking? We need to delve deeper. After all, the way we conceptualize a word dictates how we go about using it. From now on, when we think of networking, let's think of it in terms of five elements:

1) Networking is a tool.

After you enter college, you realize that as your network gets bigger, the world gets smaller. Virtually every person you could possibly want to connect with and every piece of information you could possibly want to know is just a relationship or two away. Reaching out across these relationships—that is, networking—takes both skill and persistence, but the payoff is almost always worth it. Most students allow this powerful tool to remain dormant throughout their college years. They don't take networking seriously until job-hunting season begins, but by then it is usually too late. As with any tool, you'll keep your networking skills from rusting by using them early and often.

2) Networking is fun.

That's right. Networking is fun! This is the ideal approach to take as you tread forth on the path mapped by this book and pick up new and creative ideas that help you foster new relationships. You'll find it increasingly easier to meet new people and to thrive in social scenarios. Great networkers believe that all people can help them reach their goals as long as they can find ways to reciprocate the favor. What an incredible realization! From this perspective, people all over your campus—and all over the world—are ready and willing to give you the information necessary to help you beeline toward your goals. Once you adopt this attitude, networking becomes fun. You realize that as long as there are people in the world, you always have a chance to get to wherever you're trying to go. Even if networking doesn't get easier over time, you'll certainly get better with every at bat. Through networking, you'll meet fascinating people and learn about the world and about yourself. You won't see it at first, but trust me when I say that networking can be fun and beneficial at the same time. How can you beat that?

3) Networking is a way of life.

You might be unaware of the fact that you've been networking for your entire life. You rely on your network for everything from advice on the smallest daily tasks to assistance with making life-altering choices. Your network is the place you turn to when you want an opinion on the best restaurant in a new town. You use it when you want to know where to buy your first car, where to attend college, or which job to pursue. The problem is, many people forget the importance of their networks when they get to college, despite the fact that it's even *more* important to be intentional about nurturing relationships. The people you meet, the career success you experience, and the very quality of your life will depend on the quality of your network. The better and faster you can grasp networking practices and infuse them into your everyday life, the better off you'll be.

4) Networking is necessary.

If I were a university president, I'd mandate a Networking 101 seminar for all college freshmen. Why? Because in today's world, if you don't make networking a high priority throughout college, you are guaranteed to be at a disadvantage come graduation. If we're talking about landing a job, it has been estimated that nearly 70 percent of positions in today's market are filled via internal reference. Employers are looking for recent graduates who have the kind of work experience that is virtually impossible for the average twenty-two-year-old to accumulate. If we're talking about venturing out and starting your own business, the entrepreneurship space is where only the very strong survive, and, again, the strength of your network either makes you or breaks you. The real world is a grueling one for a college graduate, and the one tool that can help you separate from the field is networking. So please, do not take building a network lightly. Take what you learn and act now. Your future depends on it.

5) Networking is a step in the right direction.

Do you consider yourself to be an ambitious, driven, goal-oriented student? Are you serious about your goals and your career dreams? Do you want to make sure that you are getting every dime out of your college experience? If you answered yes to these questions, then networking is right for you. With every key relationship made, with every conversation had, with every question answered and perspective taken into consideration, you get better and grow sharper. When you commit to building your network, you have taken one firm step in the direction of your dreams. You are on your way. Networking in college is a proactive approach to getting what you want. It's a practice for people who have found out that good things come to those who wait because the go-getters already took all the *great* things.

Dispelling the Myths: What Networking Is *Not*

To get a better understanding of what networking is, I'd like to take a good look at what networking is *not*. Sometimes all it takes is false information to deter you from doing what will benefit you greatly. To keep you from falling into this trap, let's take a look at the most common misconceptions about networking.

Myth 1: Networking is a one-way street.

Contrary to popular belief, networking is not a one-way favor, and it should never be thought of that way. "Something for nothing" does not exist in the real world. The best networkers develop the quality of giving before getting. They take pride in making networking a trust-building practice. Ironically, this mutualistic mind-set about networking will give you a clear advantage primarily because so many college students tend to do the exact opposite. They approach new relationships with a "me-first" mentality, which does them more harm than good.

Networking is a two-way street. Be mindful of the wants and needs of those with whom you network, and always offer to give before you get. People tend to go the extra mile for people who make the effort to be of assistance in some way, shape, or form. Making this a habit will benefit you tremendously in the long run.

Myth 2: Networking is only for extroverts.

The idea that introverts and shy people cannot be good networkers is 100 percent wrong. In fact, many people with introverted personalities have the knack of using their personal qualities to attract not a lot of people but the *right* people, which can lead to more powerful, more beneficial relationships. Introverts tend to flourish in one-on-one situations. They know their strengths and find networking environments that suit their personality. Networking is more than loud cocktail events with hundreds of schmoozers shuffling business cards and laughing unnecessarily hard at sandpaper-dry jokes. Networking can be authentic, personal, and incredibly beneficial to those who know how they operate best and find ways to stick to their strengths. Networking is for introverts, extroverts, and everyone in between. Yes, that includes you.

Myth 3: Networking is a numbers game.

It's not uncommon for a college student to have over a thousand Facebook friends. Of those, how many do you think this student knows well enough to ask for a personal favor? Maybe ten? We can agree that the ratio is staggeringly low. If we treat our network as we do our Facebook friends, we're in deep trouble. Collecting business cards and contact information is *not* networking. On the contrary, networking should be pointed, purposeful, and personal. As you create your network, ask yourself, why am I initiating this relationship? What are you planning to offer, and what do you hope to gain in return? Be honest when answering these questions. You might not be able to build your network quickly this way, but networking is not a numbers game. One quality relationship in which you've invested time and thought will benefit you more than ten shallow relationships combined.

Myth 4: Networking is about impressing people.

To network effectively is to make a real connection. Think about your best friend, for example. Did the two of you connect because you found each other impressive? Or did the friendship take off because you related to each other? One of the most common mistakes you'll find in networking is that people try to put on a show. Who would you rather speak with: someone who makes efforts to be relatable, or someone who makes efforts to be a standout? No one likes the guy who force-feeds poor bystanders with his accolades and accomplishments and uses self-aggrandizing speech in every other sentence. When meeting someone for the first time, the more creatively you can think about how to relate to the person rather than how to impress him or her, the better your chances of making a real connection. Ironically, being relatable is much more impressive than trying to impress. In addition, it's a key factor to networking effectively.

Myth 5: Networking is just for networking events.

Many college students are unaware of the fact that networking can be done virtually anywhere. Some of the best networking opportunities are often the least conspicuous—the local train ride into town, the basketball game, or even the wait for your mocha latte at a cafe. The idea that networking must be done in a controlled environment is a limiting belief. Allow your networking spider senses to grow sharp, and you will be ready at the drop of a dime to hold a conversation with anybody—and to open new doors for yourself at every turn.

Chapter Takeaways

- Networking is the process of cultivating goal-oriented, mutualistic relationships for the purpose of personal or professional development.

- We now live in the networked age. Never before in the modern era has relationship building played a more integral role in finding and creating the right opportunities for our career success.

- An investment in networking is an investment in your future. As a college student, there is no better time to begin building your network than *now*.

- The five most common myths about networking:

  - Myth 1: Networking is a one-way street.

  - Myth 2: Networking is only for extroverts.

  - Myth 3: Networking is a numbers game.

  - Myth 4: Networking is about impressing people.

  - Myth 5: Networking is just for networking events.

2 NETWORKING STARTS WITH YOU

Each one of us is always in danger of not being the unique and non-transferable self which he is . . . the majority of men perpetually betray this self which is waiting to be.

—Jose Ortega y Gasset, philosopher

Networking can lead you to almost any desirable end, including landing your first job and jump-starting your career. There's a caveat, though: even experienced networkers face the possibility of receiving advice that leads down the wrong path. For college students who are eager for any opportunity and are easily swayed, it is not uncommon to find themselves trekking on a career path that doesn't suit them. Their eagerness is not the problem. More likely, they end up on the wrong path because they begin the networking process with little sense of direction: *they look for help before identifying what they want and who they are.* They then go on to attach themselves to the first opportunity that comes along. In my opinion, this scenario is far too common—and far too dangerous—among college graduates.

To avoid this networking mistake, you have to find out what makes you tick. You must do the work necessary to discover your *why*. Who are you at your core, and how can you convey this message when meeting someone for the first time? The better you can convey this, the more likely you are to steer clear of advice that doesn't suit you. Your network is only as strong as your *why*, because it's your *why* that moves you. Without a sense of self-awareness, you can easily trek down the wrong path and do more damage than good to yourself and your future.

A well-defined sense of your *why* represents the difference between an effective networking system that works *for* you and a messy sea of advice that works *against* you. When you have defined your *why*, you network with confidence, clarity, and a sharp sense of direction—even if you don't know exactly what the desirable end looks like.

In order to define your *why*, begin to do the inner work that helps you to understand why you are networking in the first place.

What's Your *Why*?

Your *why* is the single motivating factor and inner-drive component that makes you and your story unique. Your *why* serves as the anchor for building your network.

A college student's *why* for becoming an engineer may originate from his time spent with his first LEGO set he played with as a child. A student may be undecided with her major, but the single motivating factor for her reaching out to working professionals in the tech industry was driven by a class on technology that piqued her curiosity. It moved her so much that she felt the need to take action.

Everyone's *why* will be different. But if you take the time to discover your *why*, mold it into your own story, and then share that story with others, you give yourself the opportunity to network with the kind of passion and clarity that others cannot deny. This will attract to you the right people and create for you the right kinds of opportunities. '

"People don't buy what you do; they buy why you do it." In his *New York Times* best seller *Start with Why,* Simon Sinek introduces to the world this fascinating concept, which has revolutionized how organizations operate today. While Sinek's primary audience may be people working at large companies, the message also proves true for you, a college student beginning your networking journey. When networking, you can build incredible relationships when you are ignited by a true sense of purpose in your pursuit of new opportunities. Whether you hope to gain an internship, a full-time job, an interview, or a referral, an individual in your network can help you only as much as you have helped yourself. What path are you on, and what kind of help do you need? What independent actions are you taking to prepare for the job you are looking to land? At the root of these questions lies the true matter at hand, the issue that you'll ideally grapple with *before* you go out and begin building professional relationships: what is your *why*? Let's take a look at how to go about answering this question.

Step 1: Begin with the *Why*, Not the *What*

People who are all about the *what* are easy to identify. They come across as boring, direct, and uninspired. When they speak about their work, it's as though they can't wait to end the conversation. On the other hand, *why* people are special. You know them even before they open their mouths. They exude confidence and give off the sense that there is a purpose in what they do. They enjoy their studies and their work, and they are not afraid to share that contagious enjoyment with others. These people find life stimulating, rewarding, and worthwhile, and this take on life is evident when you speak with them. Most of us gravitate toward *why* people.

Many college students approach their job search with a rushed and non-tactical method—that is, no method whatsoever. They do not give themselves ample time to identify their interests, passions, strengths, and weaknesses, which combine to serve as their compass for networking. When you have a deep understanding of your interests, passions, strengths, and weaknesses, you are better able to communicate about yourself effectively—an essential networking skill. These building blocks of successful networking are the first of a three-step approach to defining your *why* and networking with clarity and purpose:

Interests: What are your professional interests? What are you drawn to, including activities that you have done and activities or roles that you haven't yet tried?

Passions: What do you care deeply about? (These can be causes, current events, values, activities, groups of people, etc.) What motivates you to take action?

Strengths: What are your strengths? What have you done exceptionally in the past? What are your best personal qualities?

Weaknesses: What are your areas for improvement? What do you find most challenging?

When you answer these questions, you develop a comprehensive understanding of yourself. This, in turn, increases your confidence in your ability to network not just with people, but with the *right* people.

I'll use myself as an example. One of my passions has always been mentorship. I get a great sense of satisfaction from sharing what I know with young people in order to help them get a jump on life. Identifying this passion has allowed me to network with people who not only share my sentiment, but also have found ways to infuse the passion of mentorship into their professions. These people include teachers, coaches, and presidents of nonprofit organizations. By identifying my passion, I created a building block from which to start my professional journey. I asked myself, what kinds of jobs and industries will allow me to explore my interest in mentorship?

You might ask, what is the difference between a passion and an interest? Your interests arouse your curiosity. They are often more palpable and intellectually stimulating.

Your passions are often more heartfelt. They drive you and occupy a majority of your free time. One way to identify your passions is to answer the following question: if you could create or partake in any initiative in the world, what would that one initiative be? The answer to this question is usually driven by the emotional brain, which can tell you everything you need to know about your passions. Understanding your passions helps you better understand not only who you are now, but who you are striving to become. It allows you to communicate from a source of authenticity—and the best relationships are authentic ones.

Knowledge of your strengths is another source of confidence when networking. Are there things that most people find difficult but you can do easily? If you are a talented athlete, for example, the chances are high that you are someone who will thrive in a competitive environment. Industries like real estate, finance, and consulting are known to be competitive environments in which former athletes tend to thrive. Networking with former athletes in these kinds of industries would be a great starting point.

Pinpointing your weaknesses is something you should do for the purpose of self-awareness. Why? Because self-awareness breeds confidence. An understanding of our weaknesses can drive us in two directions. The first direction is in the direction of our strengths. A person who knows their weaknesses knows what situations to stay away from and what situations to gravitate towards. The second direction is a beeline path towards improving those weaknesses. For example, if you identify public speaking as a weakness, you may find yourself seeking public speaking groups or taking a course that would help you improve in this area. Either way you choose, by clearly identifying your weaknesses you move with more confidence. You seek out what you want—and stay clear of what you don't—with ease. And lastly, it's far better that we identify our own weaknesses before finding out from someone else!

Identifying your interests, passions, strengths, and weaknesses can do two things for you. First, it can lead you directly to the job or industry you desire, and you can then network with individuals within that industry. Second, it can attract to you like-minded individuals with whom it is easy to build rapport and to strengthen your career network. This foundation will be your internal compass as you network and as you continue to discover your *why*.

Discovering your *why* will allow you to:

- clarify your objectives

- target the individuals who can best help you

- communicate with clarity and confidence

Step 2: Formulate Your PEP Talk—Personal Elevator Pitch

Now that you've identified your *why*, it's time to tell the world who you are. Your PEP talk, or personal elevator pitch, is your message that accomplishes this task.

Everyone has some version of a PEP talk. It's the introductory statement you use in conversation when you introduce yourself to others. It is your answer to the prompt, "So, tell me about yourself." The PEP talk is critical to your networking success because it is the very first thing that comes out of your mouth. It is your opportunity to paint your self-portrait in the minds of the people you meet. The best way to create a compelling PEP talk is to take the time to figure out what it is you want other people to know about you.

A formal elevator pitch is a businessperson's concise presentation of an idea delivered in no more than fifteen seconds (the approximate duration of an elevator ride). This presentation covers all of the idea's critical aspects. Your PEP talk is similar. Whenever you find yourself in a networking situation, know that you are selling a precious idea or product—you! Who are you? What are your interests, passions, and strengths? Now is the moment when you pull from your *why* to put your authentic self on display. People with whom you network need to understand who you are and recognize your unique value by way of conversation. The way to accomplish that feat is to deliver a stellar PEP talk.

Many college students never sit down and take the time to design their personal pitch. By developing this personal introduction, you are equipping yourself with a skill set that will set you apart from your peers and allow you to effectively tell your own story. Here are four keys to keep in mind when crafting your PEP talk.

1. Tell a part of your story.

Never tell a story without making a point, and never make a point without telling a story. One of the ways to craft a compelling PEP talk is through the telling of the *introduction* to our own story. In this way, we give others the opportunity to *lean in* and learn more.

"I get a great deal of satisfaction from web design projects. In fact, I've just recently started a project working with our athletics department to improve their website."

In this way, you've given the listener the opportunity to ask more about you and learn about who you are by way of a story.

2. Lead with your strengths.

What do you do well? What position do you hold that might impress others? What do you want people to know about you? By beginning your PEP talk with your very strongest traits, you show people that you are a highly capable individual. Beginning in this way, you waste no time in presenting your best self. It's a great boost of confidence and also a great way to begin a conversation.

"The last two years as co-chair of our college pre-law organization has really allowed me to engage with professional organizations in the area and learn a great deal about some amazing initiatives."

3. Answer the question, "So what?"

"Hi, my name is Frank. I'm currently a sophomore studying economics."

Many students have the tendency to stop here with their PEP talk. My suggestion to you is to take it one just more step and answer the question, *"So what?"* Color your story by giving a compelling reason for *why* you've made the decision to attend a certain college, major in a certain department, or intern in a particular industry.

Frank may instead say something like the following.

"I've always had a fascination for the financial markets, and studying economics this year has certainly helped me grasp a better understanding of how the markets effect our daily lives."

Answering the question, "So what?" makes our PEP talk more compelling and makes us more memorable. It's a subtle change that can make a not so subtle difference when it comes to creating a PEP talk that can really spark an ongoing conversation.

4. Be yourself.

Abraham Lincoln said, "Every man is born an original, but sadly, most men die copies." He's right. When we're networking, most of us want to be like everyone else. We don't understand that the easiest people to connect to are always the best at being themselves. I remember a time when I spoke with one of my mentees before a networking event he was preparing for. "Do I laugh at jokes, or should I keep it cool?" he asked me. "How about eye contact? How long is too long?" He was overthinking the situation. I told him what I'll tell you: the most impressive people you meet will be impressive because they are comfortable in their own skin. It certainly takes practice, but if you're ever in doubt, just be yourself. At the end of the day, your PEP talk is *yours.* Be original. In doing so, you will attract the right kinds of people and relationships into your life.

Step 3: Practice Makes Perfect

You have taken the time to identify your interests, to pinpoint your passions, to sharpen your strengths, and to explore your weaknesses. You've carved out the time to formulate your PEP talk to perfection. The third and final step to prepare for your networking journey is no magic potion. Now your task is to practice. In the words of Allen Iverson, pound for pound one of the greatest point guards ever to play in the NBA, "We talkin' 'bout practice?"

Yes, we're definitely talking about practice. Practice your personal elevator pitch on everyone and anyone. The more you tell your story, the better your delivery will become. As you refine your PEP talk, you'll get a sense of what works well and what could be tweaked. You'll also find that you're more drawn to networking. Many college students dislike networking simply because they don't seek out enough chances to tell their personal story. Growing more and more comfortable with delivering your narrative and hearing your own voice is a fundamental step toward making the act of networking second nature.

Practice your PEP talk in the morning when brushing your teeth. Start small conversations in the checkout line, in the dining hall, before lecture, and wherever you find yourself with people around and time on your hands. Challenge yourself to build rapport with a stranger with as little background information as possible. Never mind how the person responds. Remember, this is your practice.

Take snippets of who you are (your *why*) and find ways to express them in your conversation.

Many of these situations will force you to step out of your comfort zone, and that's precisely what networking demands. The only way to grow comfortable with this is to practice, repeatedly, until you reach a point where you become so comfortable with yourself and your story that it won't matter what environment you find yourself in. You'll have built up the confidence and done the preparation necessary to communicate with confidence and to network with the very best of them.

Chapter Takeaways

- Networking is done most effectively from a standpoint of authenticity.

- Networking starts with you! Discover your *why* by identifying your passions, strengths, interests, and weaknesses.

- Your PEP talk (personal elevator pitch) is the pitch that you give to tell people who you are.

- When crafting your PEP talk, concentrate on four elements: 1) tell a part of your story, 2) always lead with your strengths, 3) answer the question, "So what?" and 4) be yourself.

- Your PEP talk will forever be a work in the making. Practice whenever you can on anyone who will listen! The better you get, the easier networking becomes.

Calls to Action

- What is your most prominent passion, interest, or strength? Ask three close friends or family members the same question. Find out what led them to their conclusions.

- Create your PEP talk. Write it out on a 3 x 5 index card, laminate it, and carry it with you wherever you go.

- Identify three people who you consider *why* people. These can be people you know personally or public figures. In what ways do they or their work stand out from the crowd?

3 OWN YOUR PERSONAL BRAND

*Your brand is what people say about you when
you're not in the room.*

—Jeff Bezos, CEO, Amazon

*If you're not branding yourself, you can be sure others are doing
it for you.*

—Unknown

A man walks into a hardware store in search of a nail to hang up a picture on his office wall. He approaches the store clerk and asks where he can find a one-inch nail. The clerk points the man in the direction of a bin of nails and says, "There are over a thousand one-inch nails in that bin. Choose any nail you'd like."

The man looks back at the clerk and says, "Great. But which one should I choose?"

As a college student and a young professional, you are an undifferentiated nail in a bin of a thousand nails. *You* know who you are and what makes you special, but the world doesn't have a clue what separates you from the twenty million other college students across the country.

Renowned business philosopher and author Peter Drucker calls the time we live in "the era of the three C's—accelerated change, overwhelming complexity, and tremendous competition." In 2015, of the 1.8 million people who graduated from college, only 14 percent of this group had real jobs awaiting them (AfterCollege Career Insights Survey). Based on this statistic alone, it's safe to say that Drucker is right—at least about the competition part. So how, then, do you combat the three C's? Outside of performing well in class, what can you do as a college student to ensure that you are part of that 14 percent? In order to succeed in today's competitive world, you have to make yourself visible to the right people. That involves making the transition from college undergraduate to standout applicant, from an indistinguishable nail to a unique individual who has something special to offer the world. It means taking complete control and ownership of what is called your personal brand.

Creating a personal brand helps you to carve out a niche, to gain an advantage, and to proactively jump-start your own career. You have the opportunity to take hold of your brand immediately, to attract the right crowd, and to create your own opportunities out of thin air.

So what exactly is a personal brand? A successful personal brand is a clear, effective message that you put on display every time you speak a word in person or share your thoughts online. Unlike a PEP talk, your personal brand is present even when you're not. Your personal brand is your reputation. It's what you do, and it is both your in-person and your online presence. It's what you show about who you are. Your personal brand is an essential place to begin if you want to network with confidence and to stand out from the crowd in the right way.

Let's take a look at six concepts that can help you excel when it comes to the world of self-promotion through a personal brand.

Concept 1: There Is No Shame in Self-Promotion

The first step in creating a strong, attractive personal brand is to overcome the common belief that self-promotion is a bad thing. Many of us are uncomfortable with the idea of promoting our unique talents and sharing our ideas. We see self-promotion as tooting our own horn, and we fear others will frown upon it. With this outlook, you remain safe and free from scrutiny and criticism. But no one can remain safe and opportunistic at the same time. You miss out on great opportunities when you allow yourself to remain invisible. On the other hand, when you positively promote yourself and your accomplishments, you'll increase your exposure and multiply your opportunities.

There is no shame in self-promotion. It is simply a positive way to define who you are for the greater world to see. The fact is, self-promotion is too important to you and your future to be taken lightly.

From a networking standpoint, it does you no good if you have started a blog but never have shared it with anyone. If you are the president of a club or the captain of your sports team, or if you have completed a half marathon that you trained for all semester (even though you despise running), people need to know! It is your responsibility to take 100 percent control of your image and to promote yourself and your talents creatively. Your accomplishments are part of your brand; in fact, even your unsuccessful attempts and flat-out failures can be branding-worthy material.

The working world does not reward humility. The working world is competitive, and it will be up to you to gain your advantage and to create your opportunities. No one will announce all of your accomplishments for you, and the world will not assume that you are worthy of a great job. In the end, the person who can promote you the best—who knows exactly how you wish to be seen by your peers, professors, and working professionals in your desired industry—is you!

Concept 2: Dress for Your Future

The first and most obvious aspect of your brand is your physical appearance. Most of us understand that the clothes we decide to wear on interview day are critical, but what about our attire every other day of the year? The truth is, your daily attire is very much a part of your personal brand. Your choice of appearance signals to others how to speak to you and how to receive your message. Psychology has called this 'the halo effect,' which is a cognitive bias in which our overall impression of an individual influences how we judge all other aspects of his or her character. In other words, people are more likely to think highly of you if you put more effort in how you dress. Is that a bit unfair? I'd say so. But it serves as just another helpful reminder that your image greatly impacts how the world receives you.

I learned about the negative effects of poor attire the hard way. As a student-athlete in college, I fell into the habit of wearing our team-issued athletic gear almost everywhere—in the classroom, in the dining hall, and even to semiformal on-campus events. I was comfortable in my attire, but the image I portrayed did not match the message I intended to convey. It wasn't until a close friend told me what she thought of my outfits that I realized my clothes said more about me than I said about myself! She told me the cold truth—something only close friends can do—and it completely opened my eyes. In my attire, I was viewed as a jock who was more concerned with personal comfort than anything else. In other words, the clothes I wore showed people that I simply didn't care.

Now how's that for a negative example of personal branding? I knew I had to change, and change fast. As I began to put more effort into how I dressed, something strange happened. I met and conversed with more and more people throughout the week. Over time, I felt more confident when speaking with professors because my attire was respectable. When I dressed better, I felt better, and when I felt better, I performed better. Even my grades improved over that semester. (When you dress up, you make sure not to miss a class—what's the point in dressing well if no one sees you?)

Now, do you have to wear a three-piece suit or an evening gown to your Monday morning lecture? Of course not. But we know that humans are creatures of habit. When you dress well, you project the right kind of image. People gravitate toward you and think more highly of you. Best of all, you begin to think more highly of yourself. I can't stress this point enough. Your personal brand begins with your presentation. Dress to impress! Dress for your future regardless of your audience. Do it for *you!* Hold yourself to a new standard, and watch closely as you change and your world changes with you.

Concept 3: The Networking Business Card

It's rare for college students to exchange business cards simply because most students don't have full-time jobs. As an unemployed college student, however, it's still extremely helpful to carry something that allows you to leave your name and your brand with potential members of your network. It's called the networking business card. To build your personal brand, you want to stand out in a positive way and give off a professional feel. You want people who meet you to remember who you are.

Because society has become so technology driven, traditional components of networking can seem archaic. We tend to assume that people will find out more about us online. While social media has allowed us to keep in touch, it has in some ways crippled our networking skills; we've become a bit lax in our approach to making great first impressions.

I remember attending a student career fair and watching a student basically throw a job offer out the window. After a lengthy conversation, the student told a potential employer at one of the booths to "look me up on LinkedIn." I cannot confirm, but I believe the student's chances of hearing back from that company quickly dropped from slim to none. Had he been equipped with a networking business card, he could have capped off their pleasant conversation with a physical representation of a great connection. Of the hundreds of students the company recruiter spoke with that day, how much of a difference would you suspect a networking business card would've made as she reflected back on the students who left a memorable impression?

Being a college student who gives people your networking business card is similar to being a chivalrous boyfriend who still opens car doors and pulls out chairs. Due to the simple fact that chivalry is (mostly) dead, you stand out from the crowd and brand yourself as someone who is prepared, confident, and professional.

So, what should you include on your networking business card? As a student, there is only so much information to report, but that's perfectly fine. Your name, university, and graduation year should all be included on the card. Additionally, if you have a LinkedIn account (you should!) that is up-to-date with a professional photo and a personal summary, it would be wise to include that URL as well. Lastly, it might not hurt to include your blog's website. You never know who may be interested in what you have to say!

Now, here's what *not* to include on your business card. As a college student, your interests may very well change. So, do *not* include a title tying you to a particular industry unless you are 100 percent certain that you wish to work in this industry. You do not need to pigeonhole yourself for your networking business card to be effective. Keep it simple and clean. Direct people to your professional online profile, as it is much easier to update your interests online than to remake a physical card.

Concept 4: Social Media: LinkedIn vs. Facebook

The power of social media in brand building is evident in today's world. People of all ages are finding ways to utilize these far-reaching platforms to amplify their voices for the masses. Students and young professionals with little to no work experience are finding several ways to get in front of the right crowds, to create niches, and to become go-to experts in their fields. On the Internet, the opportunities to create and communicate a respected brand are virtually limitless.

For the purpose of professional networking, LinkedIn is the best social medium for a professional to begin with. As advertised, LinkedIn is the world's largest professional network, nearing almost a half billion users around the globe. Most important, many job recruiters, company executives, and employers of all kinds are highly active on this network. Its clean and simple interface makes it a favorite landing site for working professionals. Employers use LinkedIn to survey their peers and colleagues, to keep up-to-date on industry-related news, and to scout young talent. This is where personal branding and visibility come into play.

If Facebook were a country, it would be the most populous nation on earth, with nearly 1.7 billion users as of 2016. While this may seem like the perfect platform for connecting with people and elevating your personal brand, Facebook is not the ideal outlet for a college student for several reasons. For one, you've most likely been on Facebook since your prepubescent years. Your Facebook friends include truly close friends and family members as well as people who might not even exist in real life. You've posted memes that might be funny to you and your friends but offensive to others. You might have vented once or twice in a personal status back in 2008, yet your opinions and viewpoints have changed dramatically over the years. You've grown up with Facebook, literally. We all have. And for this reason, using Facebook to connect with professionals you hope to impress may do you more damage than good.

Second, Facebook is not geared toward serious networking; it tends to be more entertainment driven. Facebook is an incredible platform for connecting with old friends, socializing, and passing the time. However, Facebook does not provide the targeted audience necessary for you to give and receive quality information with respect to building your professional brand.

LinkedIn is quite the opposite. The online professional network is designed specifically for the purpose of allowing like-minded individuals—those within the same industry or those looking for complementary skills—to find each other with ease. LinkedIn helps you identify and target small, specific groups of people with particular interests in order to build rapport and to sharpen your knowledge in those areas. Personally, my favorite feature on LinkedIn is the "interest" section, where you can search by keywords to find professional networks to join.

Whether you aspire to become a writer, a financial analyst, a coach, or a graduate student, LinkedIn's keyword search allows you to find the right people, the right networking groups, and even the right companies that will populate your news feed with career-development material. With just a few clicks, you create your own online atmosphere that keeps you up-to-date within your industry. Unlike Facebook, you can be sure that you are seeing and being seen by the right people.

Concept 5: Brandin' 'n' Bloggin'

God bless the blogging world. The blog is a tool that we've seen do wonders for people who are trying to build their careers from the ground up. Starting a blog in college is a no-brainer. From your dorm room in your pajamas, you can share your thoughts and ideas with the entire world. You can put your individuality and your expertise on display, and there is no better way to build your personal brand than to use your voice.

You don't have to be a tremendous writer to maintain a successful blog. What matters most is the energy and commitment you bring to it.

What a blog can do for you (and your brand)

In addition to being a platform for sharing original content and creative ideas, a personal blog is a resource for college students to put their interests and talents on display for the world to see. It's another viable way to show people who you are. And the more ways you have to show people who you are, the more effective your personal branding efforts will be—and the more likely you'll attract like-minded individuals.

I was offered a job interview that blossomed from one blog post. I wrote about a personal experience on the topic of networking (my niche!) and shared it on LinkedIn. An employer read the piece and thought my story would prove beneficial for high school students. He worked with a nonprofit organization and wondered if I would be interested in doing some consulting work with their program. You never know who will read your posts—put your ideas out there and give people the opportunity to find you.

Your niche: what to blog about

For starters, it's best to choose a blog topic that deeply interests you. From there, you can find individuals who are already covering hot developments in that area. If you fall short on ideas, blog about a topic that could be a great talking point for a future desirable job interview. Most bloggers' purpose is not to become famous. Rather, a blog gives you the chance to stay actively engaged with your interests.

If you are an aspiring film director, take a shot at writing about the latest films you've seen. Find other movie blogs, and leave thoughtful comments on others' film critiques. This is how you begin to build community as well as legitimacy. If you have an interest in sports, learn how to write athletic contest reviews and blog about upcoming games and high-profile athletes.

Whatever your interest—law, film, sports, finance, politics, West African culture, education, the auto industry— write about it. It will give you an opportunity as well as a reason to stay informed, to stay actively involved, and, most important, to show the world what interests you.

How often to post

You do not need to quit school and become a full-time writer to ensure that your blog works for you and helps build your brand. Blogging is effective and efficient for the mere fact that you have control over the amount of content being put out. You can blog once a week, once a month, or even sporadically. What's important is that when you meet someone, your blog serves as another tool that identifies you and helps you stand out from the majority of your peers—folks who do not have their own blog.

Author and networking expert Keith Ferrazzi put it best: "Blogs are allowing passionate individuals with good content to reach literally millions of other people. In the future, as personal branding continues to solidify itself as a mainstay in the economy, blogs will become as ubiquitous as resumes."

Concept 6: Protect Your Brand

In a recent study, the company Reppler surveyed more than three hundred hiring professionals to find out when and how job recruiters are screening job candidates on social networks. The results were astonishing.

More than 90 percent of recruiters and hiring managers have visited a potential candidate's profile on a social network as part of the screening process. 70 percent of recruiters have rejected a candidate based on content found on his or her social-networking profiles. On the other end, 68 percent of recruiters have gone on to hire a candidate based on his or her presence on those networks.

This study is eye-opening for several reasons. First, it tells us that the images and content we share online can have a negative impact on our job prospects. In today's world, employers have an opportunity to make character judgments based on what they learn about you online. Some may see it as fair practice; others may see it as a breach in privacy. Either way, it is essential to remain mindful of what your online presence says about you.

How to Lose $13 Million in One Tweet

On April 28, 2016, Laremy Tunsil, offensive tackle from Ole Miss, was waiting for the NFL commissioner to call his name. It was the NFL draft day, a high-profile event where college players wait anxiously to hear their name called and their dreams turned into reality. Draft picks can be multimillion-dollar investments. Tunsil was a highly touted player who was expected to be one of the first names called that night. In many teams' eyes, he was worthy of a major financial investment.

Just thirteen minutes before the start of the draft, the offensive tackle found himself in the midst of unwanted controversy. A video of a man wearing a gas mask and smoking from a bong was posted on his Twitter account. It wasn't confirmed that the man in the video was Tunsil, but the damage had already been done. The video was deleted almost immediately, but as we all know, once something is shared online, there's really no such thing as "delete." The image was captured by a screenshot and shared across the country within seconds. Due to this incident, many NFL team officials questioned Tunsil's character and judgment. Tumsil, once considered a top-six draft pick, dropped to the thirteenth spot. It was reported that the drop in his draft position cost Tunsil approximately $13 million in guaranteed money.

You might not be on the verge of being a superstar professional athlete, but your brand should be as important to you as Laremy Tunsil's brand was to him. Protect yourself! There is no such thing as an inside joke when it's posted online. And there is no such thing as "delete." When it comes to social media, don't make any "bonehead decisions," as my former football coach would put it. Be smart. Think twice with every status you write, every picture you take, every tweet and retweet. If you're ever uncertain about whether you should share something, let this wisdom guide you: you are what you post!

Chapter Takeaways

- To the world, you are an indistinguishable nail in a bin of a thousand nails. Developing your personal brand helps you stand out in the right way and attract the right kinds of opportunities.

- When creating your personal brand, follow these six basic steps:

  1) Understand that self-promotion is necessary. No one can promote your brand better than you can.

  2) Dress to impress. Your attire speaks just as loud as your words do.

  3) Create a personal networking business card to leave people with a piece of you wherever you go.

  4) Create a LinkedIn account in order to build your professional network.

  5) Create your own blog. Write as much or as little you want about a topic that relates to your desired industry or passion. This is a great first step to getting in the networking game and creating your own voice.

  6) Protect your brand online. Social media is a double-edged sword. Make sure you use it wisely!

Calls to Action

- Visit vistaprint.com to order as many as a hundred personalized networking business cards for under ten dollars.

- Start a personal blog on blogger.com. Select a topic relating to your niche. What interests you? What industry do you see yourself entering in the future? Write about it. Don't overthink it! Just write.

- Arrange for a professional photo to be used on your LinkedIn profile. Follow the top three individual influencers and the top three companies in your industry. Connect with individuals who express the same interests to expand your network.

- Revisit your Facebook profile. Discard and un-tag yourself from any images that will negatively impact your personal brand.

- When you're in public, dress for success! Select clothes that fit well, and don't allow casual college student attire to become the norm (athletic sweats, sweatshirts, tanks, and so on).

SECTION II.

THE TOOLS

4 THE NETWORKING E-MAIL

Tim Ferriss and the Networking Challenge

Tim Ferriss is a *New York Times* best-selling author, a successful entrepreneur, and a self-proclaimed human guinea pig. In his book *The 4-Hour Workweek*, he tells of a time when he returned to Princeton University, his alma mater, to teach undergraduates a lesson that would be of great value to them for the rest of their lives. Ferriss wanted to prove to college students that they were capable of contacting virtually anyone in the world. So, in the spring of 2005 in a lecture hall at Princeton, he challenged twenty students to contact three seemingly impossible-to-reach people: Jennifer Lopez, Bill Clinton, and J. D. Salinger. To succeed at the challenge, a student had to get at least one of these individuals to reply to three questions. Not a single student succeeded.

But Ferriss was persistent. The following year, he proposed the same challenge to a new group of Princeton students. He changed his approach slightly, however. Before making the challenge, Ferriss worked to convince students of the following belief: doing the unrealistic is easier than doing the realistic. He wanted these overly rational Ivy Leaguers to understand that virtually no one else in the country would ever attempt to contact these high-profile individuals, and therefore the chances of succeeding in this networking endeavor were ironically pretty high. Likely as a result of the mentality that Ferriss had carefully instilled, six of the students successfully completed the "impossible" task.

The students who successfully completed Ferriss's daunting networking challenge found a way to overcome the mental hurdles involved with blind networking. As it turned out, none of the winners could have completed the challenge without a fundamental understanding of the most powerful networking tool available to us: e-mail.

It's Just an E-mail . . . Right?

Even considering the recent surge in social-media outlets, SMS messaging, and other electronic forms of communication, the e-mail remains the most prevalent and most professional means of communication for people all over the world. According to the Radicati Group, Inc., in 2015, people sent and received more than 205 billion e-mails per day worldwide; 2.6 billion people actively used e-mail for correspondence. It is projected that by the end of 2019, over one-third of the world's population will be using e-mail. About 90 percent of your relationships will depend on this form of communication at some point in time while you're in college, and that number will only continue to grow after you graduate. Personally, in networking environments, I use e-mail to sustain at least three-quarters of the relationships I've developed over the years. E-mail is the cornerstone of networking.

Why is e-mail so important for college students? Essentially, it helps level the playing field. Whether an e-mail is written by the president of a company or a freshman in college, both messages will end up in the same inbox. This means that the opportunity to impress is large, yet the margin for error is slim. An effective e-mail message can open doors and knock down the barriers between any two people, regardless of age, status, or location, just as Ferriss's challenge demonstrated. This reality plays to the advantage of college students, who may lack the credentials to get in the room with a person physically but have developed a voice that commands a response by working on their e-mail–writing skill set.

E-mail Etiquette

While working with college students on a daily basis, I found that many students were either unaware of e-mail etiquette or unconcerned about the quality of their messages—or quite possibly a combination of the two. Students seemed to treat e-mailing and text messaging as the same form of communication. When I was a busy college student myself, I juggled so many tasks that when it came to writing an e-mail, I put forth the least effort necessary to get my point across. I didn't keep an e-mail address book, and I didn't think very deeply about the wide range of networking possibilities that e-mail gave me. I didn't once stop and consider all the professionals who use their e-mail on a daily basis.

In my first year working on a college campus after graduation, I asked colleagues from departments all over the university about the challenges of their work. The responses varied, but I noticed one common complaint: "Students are less than stellar when it comes to e-mail communication." Several colleagues told me stories illustrating just how casual students were with their communication—as I had been in the not-so-distant past.

"I had a student who responded to my e-mails more than two or three days after I sent them," said one colleague.

"One student kept sending me messages that misspelled my name," commented another.

College students didn't take email etiquette too seriously, and it showed.

While college administrators may show mercy when dealing with lazily written e-mails, I couldn't help but imagine how many working professionals simply moved these students' e-mails directly to their trash folders based on presentation alone. How many requests had been denied? How many networking opportunities had disappeared into thin air? And, God forbid, how many job opportunities had been lost simply because a student hadn't deemed e-mail etiquette important enough to learn?

Your e-mail presence often mirrors your presence in person, and vice versa. A sloppy introductory e-mail can damage a reputation and shut down potential opportunities.

With this in mind, it's best to approach an introductory e-mail as though it were an in-person meeting. Put your best foot forward in your networking e-mails. Not doing so can drastically cut the life span of the relationship and permanently lock doors you never even had the chance to open.

Babemagnet25@hotmail.com

Before I left my West Coast hometown for college across the country, a friend's dad wanted to make sure we kept in touch. He had an old friend who lived in New Jersey, and he wanted to connect us so that someone in the area could help me acclimate. It was an incredible gesture. The conversation went like this:

"Isaac, what's your e-mail? I'll shoot my friend a message so you two can get in touch."

"Uh . . . I think it's *a7striker@hotmail.com*."

"Okay. What's an *a7striker*?"

"Well, seven is my favorite number, and I used to play the striker position in soccer."

"Isaac, you need to change your e-mail address. You never know who you'll be e-mailing in college or, better yet, who will be e-mailing you. I don't want you to embarrass yourself."

"I've had that e-mail address since middle school! It doesn't sound too great now that you repeat it back to me. It actually sounds a bit childish. I'll get on that."

Many times, the people with whom you network will have very little information to use when trying to get a sense of who you are. Your e-mail address is one of those pieces of data, and it's often the first thing people see. An e-mail address can very well be the difference between receiving a thoughtful reply and receiving no reply whatsoever.

When you choose your e-mail address, pick something that represents you well. Don't allow yourself to be viewed like the *a7strikers*, the *babe_magnets*, or the *surfer_girls* of the world. Choose an e-mail address that is simple, respectable, and long-lasting. The mistake of selecting an inappropriate address may sound trivial, but it could be fatal to your networking opportunities.

The Power of *.edu*

One of the most valuable gifts your college will give you is your e-mail address: *name@school.edu*. With this address, you have officially been stamped, and your personal brand has been partially launched. This is an incredible boost in the arena of networking. Attached to every e-mail you send is your university's name, making you a doubly powerful force to be heard and respected (or at least not trashed immediately). You are now a recognizable and competitive force when you enter someone's inbox. Regardless of the school you attend, the *.edu* informs e-mail recipients of your status as an individual backed by a respected institution. In other words, anderson@gmail.com looks okay, but anderson@utexas.edu is much more professional and appealing. Being a part of the *.edu* family gives you the opportunity to reach out to others with some networking power for the first time in your life.

And the power doesn't stop there. As a college student, you are in the prime position to network with the overwhelming majority of working professionals. Why? Because virtually everyone you meet can relate to you. When you reach out, they know why you're reaching out before you say a word. They understand the *"I don't know what I'm doing, but I'm trying to learn and grow"* college experience. The *.edu* gives you leverage to take advantage of this unique position. Connect with multiple professionals and ask them for advice. Look for interesting people to learn from, and find out if you can become their mentee. There is tremendous networking power in being a novice, and utilizing a *.edu* e-mail address helps you maximize that power.

Fundamentals of the Networking E-mail

A networking e-mail is a first-time e-mail request sent for the primary purpose of turning a stranger into a resource. The sender hopes to gain knowledge from a more experienced person and to build a genuine bond in the process. Networking e-mails are usually requests for advice or assistance via e-mail correspondence, a phone call, or a conversation over coffee.

A networking e-mail is all about communication skills—in this case, your ability to structure a written message. An effective networking e-mail is professional in its presentation, concise in its language, and clear in its purpose. With these elements in place, you'll start each potential long-term relationship off on the right foot.

Let's take a look at the three components of a networking e-mail: the subject line, the body, and the signature.

The subject line

Besides your e-mail address itself, the quality of your subject line is the single determining factor of whether your e-mail will be opened or ignored. In the industry of e-mail marketing, large businesses pay millions of dollars to find creative ways to stand out in an inbox. These marketing professionals spend most of their brainpower on crafting the perfect subject line. Without that click from the receiver of the e-mail, businesses miss out on another opportunity to present more of their products and messages to a customer. When it comes to networking e-mails, think of yourself as a business. You want to craft a subject line that guarantees you the click. Here are four strategies for creating the right subject line:

1) **Ask a specific question:** *Student seeking advice on ____. Available for brief phone call?*

2) **Refer to specific work of email recipient.** If the email recipient has written a book, blog, or other kind of relatable content, it never hurts to offer up a specific question referencing the work in your subject line. An individual is very likely to open a message from someone who has shown interest in their work. *'Question about Name of Book here'.*

3) **Provide a one-line summary.** When connecting with a high-profile individual, get straight to the point. Sometimes a one-line summary is the most effective way

to get an immediate response: *Engineering undergrad seeking insight on master's program.* Summaries can be dry, but they often result in a quicker response than the heartfelt, long-winded approach.

4) **Mention a mutual friend.** If a mutual friend or contact referred you to your networking target, make sure to mention that person in the subject line: *Reaching out via Mary Johnson '95.*

The body

Now that your excellent subject line has convinced your targeted recipient to open your e-mail, you want to make sure that the body of the message is clear, concise, and professional. Let's break it down into four easy elements.

1) **Greeting.** A great rule of thumb is to be formal until you're given the heads up to do otherwise. In your greeting, stick to the appropriate honorific titles—Dr., Mr., Mrs., Ms., Prof., and so on. While the recipient may prefer to be called by his or her first name, sticking with formalities is a great way to show respect and to bring you that much closer to a favorable answer to your request. Starting with *"Hey Joe,"* especially when you have never met Joe, will likely come off as overly informal and presumptuous.

2) **Who are you? How'd you find me? Why are you reaching out?** If you can find a way to answer these three questions in your first few sentences, you are on your way to writing a succinct and powerful networking e-mail. Here are two examples:

Dear Mr. Williams:

My name is Charles Hanks, and I am currently an engineer at Princeton University. As a junior interested in the _____ industry, I read your book, which made such an impact on me that I had to reach out to you personally and say thank you.

Dear Professor Dryer:

My name is Susan Davidson, and I am currently a freshman at Cal Poly. After reading about your vast experience in the consulting industry after getting a sociology degree—a department I am leaning toward—I am hoping to pick your brain about how that decision played a role in your professional career and beyond.

3) **Preferred time line.** One of the most common mistakes college students make in a networking e-mail is failing to present a preferred time line. Here's what it looks like:

Would you be available for a 10–15 minute phone call in the next month? If the dates below do not work for you, please let me know, as my schedule is very flexible.

How does next Friday (October 10) work for you? I am usually available in the evenings.

Networking targets appreciate requests that are specific and painstakingly clear. When in doubt, remember that specificity gets met with specificity, generality with generality. A time line creates a bit of urgency—and with zero urgency, you'll get zero response. Offering one, two, or even three specific date and time suggestions shows that you are serious about your request, therefore boosting the likelihood that your target will respond seriously. It is also a great sign of professionalism and organization, two qualities that are great to display when initiating a potential long-lasting relationship.

4) **Repeat request and thank in advance.** The closing of your e-mail should consist of a paraphrase of your request, followed by a thank-you for your target's time and future response. A repeated request serves as a gentle reminder and a respectful way to convey urgency:

Thank you again for considering my request for a phone call. If any of the proposed times do not work, please don't hesitate to suggest a time that works for you. I look forward to hearing from you in the near future.

The Signature

Your e-mail signature is the finishing touch to your masterpiece, and it's important to make sure that your final touch is a special one. A small fraction of college students consistently send networking e-mails. And of the wise students who *do* send these messages consistently, only a special few use a unique signature to stand out in a congested inbox.

An e-mail signature should include your name, university name, and telephone number. In addition, you can provide the link to your professional networking (LinkedIn) profile and even a small professional photo of yourself. Should recipients want to find out more about you, they can use the link located in your signature to visit your online profile. This kind of transparency can serve as a great icebreaker even before you and your target meet.

You have several options for creating your e-mail signature. Fiverr.com, Hubspot.com, and the "e-mail signature" iPhone app are just a few resources to try. For less than a five-dollar investment, your e-mail signature can drastically change your online presence and give you that edge you're looking for.

So those are the big three: the subject line, the body, and the signature. By mastering these components of the networking e-mail, you will grow more and more comfortable reaching out to virtually anyone with an e-mail address. The more networking e-mails you send, the better you'll get. A great e-mail can be the difference between an ignored request and a job interview. A great e-mail can separate you from your peers and allow you to connect with working professionals all over the world. Just ask Tim Ferriss.

What *Not* to Do

Now you know what to do. But should you ever feel tempted to stray from the basics, here are four things never, ever to do when sending networking e-mails.

1) Do not send mass e-mails.

Never send mass e-mails when networking. Mass e-mailing is comparable to standing at the entrance of a networking event and handing out your networking card to everyone who walks through the door. It can be seen as classless, tasteless, and rude. As the saying goes, if you try to catch them all, you'll most likely end up catching none at all. The most effective networking e-mails are personal and well crafted—neither of which applies to a mass e-mail. When you send a networking e-mail, make sure it's for one targeted recipient.

2) Do not use the phrase 'To Whom It May Concern."

Never send an e-mail (or resume, or anything for that matter) with the salutation "To Whom It May Concern." This greeting may have worked in the distant past, but in today's world it screams, "I'm too lazy to find out whom this e-mail concerns." If you don't know the appropriate recipient of your e-mail, you shouldn't expect someone else to figure it out on your behalf. There is no crime in sending cold networking e-mails—that is, unsolicited messages to a target with whom you have no prior connection. But at the very least, you should do the research necessary to determine the correct recipient. If you don't know—or if you don't want to take the time to find out—it's a telltale sign that you shouldn't be sending the e-mail.

3) Do not address multiple topics in a single networking e-mail.

Remember that clarity is key. You never want recipients to be confused about what you are requesting or how they should respond. One of the best ways to ensure this clarity is to address only a single topic when writing a cold networking e-mail. The rules can change for subsequent e-mails, but to begin, keep your message as singular and concise as possible.

4) Do not deliver a "no" over e-mail.

This "don't" might come as a bit of a surprise. It's a personal preference of mine, but I feel it is a great rule to live by. If someone has sent you an invitation or has offered you a friendly gesture over e-mail, do not e-mail a negative response. E-mails are for yeses, compliments, and pleasant exchanges. No matter how well written, an e-mail rejection can be interpreted as disingenuous and coldhearted.

Let's say a friend e-mails you to invite you out for coffee this week, but you won't be able to make it. While it may be easier to shoot back a reply over e-mail, do your friend (and yourself) a favor and give him a quick phone call. Genuinely thank him for the invitation *first,* and give your reasonable explanation for the rain check *second.* A human voice can convey sincerity while rejecting an offer. An e-mail, on the other hand, cannot.

Chapter Takeaways

- Over 205 billion e-mails are sent and received in the world every single day. E-mail is the single most effective networking tool you have.

- A poorly constructed e-mail can obliterate opportunities you never even knew existed. Follow the dos and don'ts in order to communicate with clarity and to let your networking targets know they're dealing with a true professional.

Calls to Action

- Choose a respectable personal e-mail address. A variation of your name is the safest and best way to go. (Stay away from nicknames, inside jokes, and your favorite TV shows.)

- Visit fiverr.com to create your own unique e-mail signature. This feature will cost you ten dollars at the most.

- Browse your inbox and identify three e-mails that grab your attention. What makes these e-mails so effective? Evaluate the subject line, the body, and the overall presentation.

- Revisit the last three e-mails you sent. How would you compare the subject line, body, and overall presentation to the e-mails you identified and evaluated previously? Identify one takeaway that you can apply to composing e-mail messages in the future.

- Using the e-mail templates provided in this chapter, send a networking e-mail today. Don't delay—sometimes "later" becomes "never."

5 THE ART OF NETWORKING

The Five Key Ingredients of a Great First Impression

We've all heard the phrase, "You never get a second chance to make a first impression." But just how important is that first impression when it comes to networking?

Psychological research from the past three decades has proven time and time again that our subconscious mind makes long-lasting judgments about new people and situations within seconds of being exposed to them. In fact, some researchers have gone as far as to claim that our first impressions form in the first seven seconds of interaction!

Take the incredible study conducted by the social psychologist Nalini Ambady. While at Tufts University, Dr. Ambady asked a group of brand-new first-year graduate students to complete written evaluations of their professor. These evaluations were based singularly on watching a fifteen-second muted video clip of their professor teaching a class. After the students had worked closely with this professor for two years, Dr. Ambady had them do another evaluation so that she could compare how students perceived their professor before and after two years of close contact. The results showed that students' evaluations after two years of work were virtually identical to their initial impressions. Two years of personal interaction made no difference in their initial impressions of the lecturer—the impressions that formed after a fifteen-second clip.

So, how does this study apply to the world of networking? For one, we know that first impressions are at the core of networking. When we walk into a room, attend an event, meet a new person, and strike up conversation, the power of the first impression is on full display. Our ability—or inability—to come across as warm, welcoming, competent, and confident is what dictates not only how people view us in that moment but also what they think of us when our conversation ends.

College will present you with several social situations in which first impressions are important, but one kind of event, if approached in the right way, can help you grow your network especially effectively. It is what I call a quasi-networking event—a social gathering held on campus that allows undergraduates to socialize with working professionals, alumni, and college administrators. Most students miss out on the networking opportunities built into these social events. How can you make sure you don't miss out on these opportunities?

During my sophomore year in college, I received an invitation to the fall sports luncheon. This annual event, which was held on campus, marked the ending of the fall sports season and served as a formal celebration of achievements and accolades. As a student, I never really looked at the event with networking eyes; I didn't think of it as anything other than a free meal. Looking back, I realize what the event really was: an incredible opportunity for a young pup like myself to network, to find mentors, to build relationships, and to spend rare quality time with working professionals. It was a chance to meet new people and to grow more comfortable in unconventional networking environments.

Every college across the country holds quasi-networking events at which alumni and local working professionals are encouraged to come to campus and to interact with current students. Whether it is a luncheon like the one I attended, an alumni/ae event, or a homecoming celebration, these opportunities are networking gold mines for you. Your first job may very well be one smile, one handshake, or one engaging conversation away.

To take full advantage of these networking events, you need to be able to make a knockout first impression. A great first impression in a networking environment can be the difference between a conversation fizzing out or taking flight. A strong first impression is the prerequisite to a *real* conversation, and a real conversation is the prerequisite to the uncovering of a great opportunity.

Quasi-networking campus events are littered with the right kinds of people who can help you build your network. Many of them not only *can* help you, but also *want* to help you! When alumni/ae and graduates of other universities visit a college campus, they understand that students are looking to plant seeds for their future. The environment is set up for you to capitalize on these opportunities. Your responsibilities are to show up and perform! Let's look at five key elements that ensure you are exercising your first impression power.

1) The power of dress

Your attire says a lot about you without your uttering a word. Furthermore, it communicates what you think about the event you are attending. Regardless of the event's degree of formality, dress sharp. Do not try to match your peers so that you'll fit in; this is your time to stand out. Remember, *you* are the one searching for people who will offer you that diamond-in-the rough opportunity. Regardless of how dynamic the conversation, if your clothing isn't sharp, you'll find it difficult to convert that conversation into a long-term relationship or a concrete lead. Dress for success, and watch how differently you are approached wherever you go.

2) The power of a smile

> A smile says, "I like you. You make me happy. I am glad to see you."
>
> —Dale Carnegie

> Don't just smile back. Smile first.
>
> —Isaac Serwanga

Your smile is your brand. We smile to show acceptance, to express pleasure, and, most important, to build a real connection. You'd be amazed to discover how many people are unaware of 1) the impact of their smile as it relates to first impressions, and 2) their smile's potential long-term impact on others' perceptions of their personality, charisma, and even competency.

It is no coincidence that people in the most prominent positions in our society tend to be quick to offer up a welcoming smile. Whether it be the CEO of a company or the school principal, these positions carry the responsibility of meeting new people nearly every day. High-ranking individuals understand that the best way to greet new people is with a smile. President Obama, for instance, can offer up his trademark million-dollar smile at the drop of a dime. It should come as no surprise when you see powerful people using the power of a smile to their advantage whenever possible.

Offering up a genuine smile when you meet new people sends several messages—all positive—that will open the door for positive exchange. People are more likely to connect with you, to engage with you, and to think highly of you. As someone once told me, a smile is the real hello before we say hello. A genuine smile is the easiest way to give someone a warm welcome before even uttering a word.

The coffee shop smiling experiment

As a human guinea pig, I decided to try an experiment to illustrate the effectiveness of a smile and its power to lead to deeper, friendlier human interactions. When writing this very book at a local coffee shop, I made a concerted effort to greet ten individuals in the span of two hours. I looked at each person, said hello with a nod but no smile, and returned to my work. Eight out of ten individuals verbally replied, "Hello."

One week later, I repeated the experiment. I sat at the same table at the same time of day. I even wore the same outfit for the sake of consistency. Nearly everything was identical, except for one slight alteration: this time around, after saying hello, I gave each person my most genuine smile before putting my head down and continuing to pound away at my keyboard. Adding the smile felt a bit strange at first—and then another strange thing happened. The first five individuals verbally said hello, as my first round of subjects had. But this time, unlike round one of my experiment, four out of five people felt compelled to converse with me. They asked me how my day was going and wanted to know what I was working on. Of these individuals was a man named Paul. After I told him about this book, Paul mentioned to me that he had been a college professor for over twenty-five years. He loved the concept of teaching students how to network in college. Paul offered to introduce me to a few administrators at the community college where he had once taught so that I could share the book with their students.

This is just one example of the power of a smile. The fact is, you never know where one conversation can lead you. Whenever you're in doubt, remember that a genuine smile is the first step in a great conversation. From there, the possibilities are endless.

3) The power of expectancy

> *Every man I meet is my superior in some way, and in that I learn from him.* —Ralph Waldo Emerson

When you adopt Ralph Waldo Emerson's outlook on the world, networking becomes quite easy. Instead of being hesitant about entering a conversation, you expect to come away with something of value. But what does it mean to be expectant? To be expectant is to approach a conversation with the intent of learning, as Emerson did. Think about a child before she opens her Christmas gift. Her excitement is so intense that it's contagious. She expects something great, and it shows.

Networking is no different. People who *expect* to meet great people often bring the greatness out of the people they meet. Many people who dislike networking believe that strangers are often cold toward them. When meeting new people, they expect the worst from themselves and others—and they almost always get what they expect. Meeting someone new is an event to be met with a positive sense of expectancy. You can never underestimate where one conversation can lead you. That's the beauty of networking! Approach every conversation with the expectation that you'll make a terrific connection. More than likely, you'll get exactly what you expect.

4) The power of body language

> *Your body communicates as well as your mouth.*
> *Don't contradict yourself.* —Unknown

We all know our own stories, but how much thought do we give to how well we listen to someone else's? Listening is as much physical as it is auditory. Studies have shown that 80 percent of interpersonal communication is nonverbal. That is, what we say in conversation is minimally important compared to how we deliver our message, as well as how we receive the other person's. Knowing this, it becomes critical that we pay attention to what we are saying with our bodies as well as our words. Being mindful of the many ways to communicate can help us become better communicators and more effective networkers. Our eye contact, gestures, and even facial expressions tell people who we are even more effectively than our words do.

When it comes to improving communication through body language, focusing on just a few of your deficiencies can make a world of difference. For instance, you will convey confidence, poise, and competency—all the ingredients of an incredible first impression—by maintaining decent posture, sustaining eye contact when both talking and listening, and keeping your fidgety movements to a minimum.

5) The power of intriguing open-ended questions

When you're having a conversation with a networking target, remember this last but critical piece of information: great answers impress, but great questions connect. A well-delivered, well-thought-out question between strangers is the quickest way to break the ice. A great question takes time and consideration. It's the easiest way to show someone that you are keenly interested in what it is he or she has to say. Dale Carnegie sums it up best: "The easiest way to be interesting is to be interested." Show interest in the people you talk to. By conjuring up great questions, you give people the chance to show you just how interesting they are.

The best types of conversational questions are open-ended. Replace the dull question "What do you do?" with "Tell me what you like most about your work." Instead of asking an alumnus, "When did you graduate?" give him the opportunity to tell a story by asking, "What did you do during the summer following graduation?"

When you ask open-ended, creative questions, you give people the chance to break away from scripted, mundane, all-too-familiar networking answers. You give them the floor to open up and to elaborate, which most often elicits unique answers and thus a dynamic conversation. A great open-ended question is the quickest way for you to break the ice and to leave an unforgettable impression on all those who cross your path.

The Informational Interview

A genuine smile, a respectable outfit, an expectant positive attitude, positive body language, and a handful of intriguing open-ended questions—these are the five key elements of a great first impression at a networking event. So, what's next? The purpose of a networking event is to find the people and relationships that can be of use to you and to your future. The follow-up to these events usually comes in the form of an informational interview.

By formal definition, an informational interview is an arranged meeting or conversation in which you, the potential job seeker, seek advice from a working professional in an industry that you'd like to learn more about. It's a great way for college students to learn about specific jobs or industries straight from the horse's mouth.

In fact, in a recent survey conducted by an independent research firm for Accountemps and involving more than 2,200 chief financial officers from a sampling of companies in twenty of the largest metropolitan areas, 84 percent of respondents said that when someone impresses them in a meeting, it's likely they'll alert that person to job openings at the company.

The informational interview is an opportunity to get a real-world perspective from someone who has trekked on your path and now occupies a role you could potentially see yourself playing down the road. It can serve as an incredible networking tool for people just starting out and getting their feet wet.

The beauty of the informational interview is its multifunctionality. Whether you are preparing for an upcoming job interview, looking to gather knowledge about an industry of interest, or simply planting employment seeds for the future, the interview's format allows you to use it whichever way works best for you. First, let's walk through three ways to effectively utilize an informational interview.

1) The targeted informational interview: Harness the power of internal referrals

To use the informational interview in a particularly strategic way, request a targeted interview. A targeted informational interview is conducted with someone who may have valuable information about a particular position or company that you've targeted in advance. For example, let's say a certain company has a summer internship program that you'd like to learn more about before you apply. After conducting some research, you arrange to speak with someone who works at the company—or at least within the same industry—and will have tremendous insight about the internship program as well as the application process. This individual could be an alumnus/a, a friend of a friend's parent, or someone you met more than a year ago. It could even be a stranger. Regardless, the motive and purpose do not change. The purpose of the arranged call is to gather insight and information that you cannot access with a Google search.

Here are some sample questions to ask in the above scenario:

- How did you get into this line of work?

- How can I best prepare for the internship's application process?

- What are the intern's day-to-day responsibilities?

The ideal questions will give you a real feel of the job, the company, and the industry in general. This kind of information is invaluable when it comes from a subjective point of view. Too many college students walk blindly into their jobs and internships with the assumption that their experience will be exactly what was listed in the job description. The targeted interview is your secret weapon. It's your cheat code. But like any cheat code, it's often difficult to get your hands on.

Most college students fail to land targeted interviews because they give up when their first contact doesn't pan out. It takes effort to find ways to contact people, and this effort scares off the majority of the crowd. It's almost always worth it to go the extra mile and exhaust your resources, however. Networking always works in favor of those who are persistent and unrelenting.

My NCAA targeted informational interview

In the spring of my senior year at Princeton, a job with the NCAA caught my eye. The position was as a coordinator working primarily on the men's March Madness basketball tournament. While the position had already been filled for that year, I sought to arrange a targeted informational interview with someone at the NCAA in order to gain some insight about the position and, more important, the interview process for the future. After tapping into every group association I knew, I found an NCAA employee who was an alumnus of my university and a former student-athlete like me. These two common links were enough to connect us in a significant way. After a few e-mails, we scheduled a fifteen-minute chat over the phone. After a small chat about Princeton athletics, I asked questions about his journey to the NCAA, the organization's culture, what it was like to live in Indianapolis, the sports industry, and the differences between college and professional athletics. The conversation was going well, so I delved into *why* I wanted to work for the NCAA, including my background and the strong influence of athletics on my life.

Almost a year later to the day, I was flying out to Indianapolis for my interview for the same job that had caught my eye. Over 650 people had applied for the position. When I arrived, the first sentence out of every one of my interviewers was something close to the following: "Isaac, we've heard such great things about you." It just goes to show that one great conversation can go a long way.

My exhaustive preparation for the interview process allowed me to perform at my best in the all-day interview. Yet the other applicants had prepared exhaustively too. It was the targeted informational interview I had arranged nearly a year earlier that made just enough of a difference. It gave me an internal referral and bought me the invaluable gift of familiarity. My advantage over the other applicants may have been slight, but in a competitive environment, a slight advantage is what led to a job offer.

2) The nontargeted informational interview: Practice! Practice! Practice!

Informational interviews can be uncomfortable, awkward, and nerve-wracking. The only way you can improve with these interviews is by scheduling more interviews! A nontargeted informational interview is a scheduled call made with a working professional solely for the purpose of relationship-building and gathering generic information about an industry or steps toward a particular career path. Beforehand, you'll be asking yourself all kinds of questions: "How do I present myself? Is it better to be honest about my weaknesses and lack of experience, or do I focus on my strengths and project confidence? Do I ask a lot of questions, or should I elaborate on my accomplishments?" If anyone has ever given you an outright proven method to acing a nontargeted informational interview, I'm here to let you know that such a magic method doesn't exist.

The truth is, every conversation will be somewhat different from the next because the people will be different and the circumstances will change. Therefore, the best way to improve your approach to an informational interview is to practice over and over again.

To ensure that you get the practice you need, try setting an informational interview schedule. Establish periodic times for reaching out to people and holding these conversations throughout the academic year. With nontargeted informational interviews, remember that it's best to begin with no specific result in mind. While this approach may sound unusual, it's a terrific way to practice for real job interviews in the future. Informational phone interviews also give you an opportunity to practice your PEP talk, a topic we discussed in chapter 2.

A baseball player who wants to improve his hitting can try every exercise in the book outside of playing baseball. But at the end of the day, in order to improve, he needs more at bats—he needs more swings. For a college student who wants to build a strong network, the non-targeted informational interview is what gives you more at bats. The more opportunities you can create for yourself to converse with working professionals, the more you practice telling strangers who you are and what you want to do with your life. And the more relationships you build throughout your time in college, the sharper and brighter your future becomes. As in sports, you can practice all the drills, but the best way to improve your game is to play the game more often.

Do not wait until you need a job to begin reaching out for information and building strategic relationships. Make informational interviews a regular practice, and watch as your professional communicative skills progress over the course of your time in college.

3) Extend your network: Plant the employment seed

Benjamin Franklin once stated, "He that has once done you a kindness will be more ready to do you another, than he whom you yourself have obliged." This maxim was so powerful that it became a psychological phenomenon, adopted by social psychologists and now known as the Ben Franklin effect. Franklin was known as a networking mastermind. He lived by this personal maxim and accomplished many of his lofty goals by befriending others.

An informational interview is the Ben Franklin Effect in action. You provide people with the opportunity to help you. In turn, the seeds that you plant—which, in most cases, are seeds of employment, can come back to help you in a big way.

As your network grows, don't be alarmed if you don't see concrete results right away. Some of these relationships won't reveal their value for weeks, months, or even years. Simply by extending your network, you plant the seeds of future benefit. You give yourself a chance to gather new information, and to take positive steps toward the future you want.

Preparing for an informational interview: The five rungs of research

As you may suspect, the success of an informational interview depends heavily on your preparedness. A simple method to follow is called the five rungs of research. Constructing this guide prior to your informational interview will give you an outline from which you can craft questions and create a checklist to ensure you are covering all the essentials. Think of this as your bumper-bowling guide—let it keep you from throwing gutter balls until you've had enough practice to give it a go on your own:

1) **Industry.** When preparing for an informational interview, one-fifth of your research should concentrate on the industry you want to learn about. Having at minimum a brief understanding of the overall industry will give you the ability to speak on this generally and allow you to construct some educated questions to inject into the conversation. Nine times out of ten, a Google search will suffice.

2) **Company.** The next 20 percent of the research you conduct should concern your target interviewee's company. The company's website (found with a simple Google search) will probably contain all the material you would need for an informational interview. A review of the company's size, departments, and mission will help you create a few informed questions for your conversation.

3) **Position.** If you've scheduled a targeted informational interview, it's essential that you know as much as the Internet can tell you about the position that interests you

as well as the company. Your objectives in the targeted interview are to gain information and, most important, to come off as a highly prepared candidate with hopes of getting your name in circulation. To achieve this, it's imperative that you do thorough research on the position and ask specific questions.

4) **Individual.** An informational interview is essentially a conversation. Do the research necessary to, again, carve out a few personal questions that will advance your conversation. What is your interviewee's academic background? How long has he or she worked for the company? What was his or her first job out of college? The answers to these questions can provide helpful talking points and lead to additional well-crafted questions.

5) **The PEP talk.** This is the only rung of research that involves you answering questions about yourself. The PEP talk is your personal elevator pitch. Simply put, you'll need to rehearse your answers to the following prompts:

- Tell me about yourself.

- Where do you see yourself in three to five years?

- What draws you to this industry, company, and/or position?

Of all the research you do, the PEP talk rung is by far the most important. Your answers to these questions will change (and hopefully develop!) with every informational interview. Practicing and rehearsing your PEP talk is the most beneficial component of conducting informational interviews.

With every informational interview you conduct, you'll learn about a particular industry, profession, or person. You'll also learn a great deal about yourself. You'll grow more confident in your answers to common networking questions. After the first five informational interviews, you will see a drastic change in your comfort level when discussing your future. You will begin to refine and clarify your answers. This is the kind of invaluable personal growth that comes with the habitual practice of informational interviewing. No class will teach you this—you've got to do it on your own!

When things go wrong

Following the five rungs of research will prepare you to knock your interview out of the park. But things can always go wrong, so we hope for the best and prepare for the worst. You can follow all of the recommended steps to a tee, yet letdowns can still occur. During your networking adventures, someone will most likely fail to show up for a meeting that you arrange. Someone will probably cancel the conversation, perhaps without explanation. A few might be short, brusque, or seemingly unimpressed by your questions. And some will inevitably give you useless or illogical advice. As you become more confident and reach out to more and more people, there will always be a bad apple or two. And that's okay. Do not let this discourage you from networking! Understand that this is just part of the process. Here are some troubleshooting tips:

1) **When people cancel or reschedule.** When you begin networking, you will quickly learn that people's schedules are unpredictable. A contact's reason for

canceling or rescheduling an information interview could be real or imaginary. I've heard it all, and some are more believable than others. One contact wrote, "Isaac, my business conference ran over by a few hours, and I'm a bit behind schedule. May we reschedule for next week? Either Monday or Wednesday evening EST—let me know." Another gave no reason at all: "Hey—So sorry! Can we reschedule?" The worst was receiving no heads up whatsoever.

2) Regardless of how your networking contact handles this situation, try to focus on yourself in these situations. Are you upset? Of course you are. But these are the best moments for you to practice displaying poise, gratitude, and an incredible attitude toward the uncertainties that life throws your way. Do your best to remain positive and flexible.

3) In the event of a cancellation, let the contact know that you understand his or her situation and that you are thankful for the note. Offer a date or two for a future meeting. If it was a scheduled in-person meeting, could a conversation over the phone suffice? Find ways to be flexible, and remain positive. This mind-set will go a long way for you as you continue to develop your network.

4) **When people give bad advice.** Remember two things. One, not every piece of advice that comes your way will be great advice. And two, free advice is sometimes worth more than what you pay for. For these reasons, it is imperative to keep in mind that at the end of the day, the choice to act is yours. What you decide to do after gathering the relevant information is up to you. No one knows you and your situation as well as you do.

The great thing about networking is that you only need to be right once. You are not out to land *every* job and capitalize on *every* opportunity. Networking allows you to build great relationships and hit home runs from time to time, but striking out comes with the territory. Regardless of the outcome, every at bat teaches you something valuable. I recall the following truth every time I decide to attempt something that scares me: There is no such thing as a loss. You either win or you learn.

The Art of Coffee Talks

Talk to someone about themselves and they'll listen for hours.
—Dale Carnegie

It's the end of summer, and school will be starting up again in no time. After a relaxing but not-so-productive two and a half months, you come to the harsh realization that next summer needs to look incredibly different if you are going to prepare yourself for the real world. Lazy-day summers spent at home lounging on the couch, browsing the web, and catching Pokémon will no longer be acceptable. You need to find an internship that offers you real work experience and a job that doesn't pay in monopoly money.

After asking close family members and friends for advice, your mom reminds you that she has a good friend who works for a consulting company in the large metropolitan area just fifteen miles north of your university. You and your mom's friend exchange a few e-mails and agree to meet up. She'll be near campus in the fall and would love to, as she puts it, "catch up and chat over coffee."

What is a coffee talk?

You have just confirmed your first coffee talk. In any industry, the coffee talk is by far the most effective method for working professionals to build rapport in a one-on-one setting. A coffee shop or local eatery makes for a comfortable, easygoing environment. While you're in college, it's best to approach every coffee talk with a working professional as an informal job interview before what will hopefully become an actual interview. It's a chance for you to practice your conversational skills in an informal setting, to organically build your network with industry professionals, and, most important, to plant the seeds for future employment opportunities.

How coffee talks benefit you

College students gain several distinct advantages from coffee talks. These advantages come as a result of the experiences you encounter, the skill sets you build and sharpen, the opportunities you create, and the people you meet. No college course can substitute for the real-world, practical lessons that come from coffee talks. Coffee talks are designed to prepare you for life after graduation. They improve your ability to leave a great impression on people in one-on-one settings, to ace job interviews, and to locate job prospects.

Let's start with one-on-one communication skills. In a recent study by the Harvard Business Review, senior level executives rated communicative skills above all when it came to offering job promotions to employees. I would bet that these findings could be extended to the importance of communication during job interviews. Your ability to communicate effectively is directly related to your success, especially in your postgraduate life.

Seldom will you have the chance to speak about your future while in college. Many college students are so focused on grades and what's happening on campus that they wait until interview time comes around to perfect their story. They wait until the pressure is on and the stakes are incredibly high. Coffee talks give you the opportunity to clean up your delivery as you express who you are, what you've accomplished, what interests you, and where you see yourself headed in the future. During these conversations you'll work out the kinks, slowly build your communication skills, and learn how to effectively deliver your personal story.

The second benefit of coffee talks is that they can find you a job. Someone who is in a position to help you generally wants to get to know you first. A great coffee-shop conversation can open the door for great referrals, potential work opportunities, and, in rare cases, even an on-the-spot job offer. If you can get yourself in front of a decision maker—or someone close to the decision maker—you're at an advantage in the interview process before it has even begun. Several studies have shown that people who begin the interview process having already made a personal connection with someone within the organization have a considerable advantage over those who have not. The coffee talk is the ultimate platform for making a personal connection. The more opportunities you give decision makers to get to know who you are, the stronger the bond grows.

The third benefit of coffee talks is that they deepen your networking relationships. Networking takes several forms, each serving its own purpose. Breadth networking refers to networking that happens in environments that encourage several short and sweet interactions, often ending with an exchange of a card and contact information. Large networking events and industry-specific conferences are examples of breadth opportunities. They allow you to get your feet wet and to widen your network.

Breadth networking events often serve as the precursors to what we call depth networking. Depth networking takes place mostly in small groups or during one-on-one conversations, such as the coffee talk. Depth networking should take place more often than breadth networking only after you begin to carve out specific goals or desired outcomes (such as a particular job, an internship referral, or a networking contact within a specific company or industry). The more depth networking you do, the better your chances of finding the right job or allowing the right job to find you.

How to prepare for coffee talks

So you've scheduled your very first coffee talk. Congratulations! Here are five pointers to help you prepare and network like a true professional.

1. The law of familiarity

Let's refer to the scenario described at the beginning of this section. Your mom's friend, who works at a consulting company near your college, wants to meet at a local off-campus coffee shop. Now, let's be honest: how often do you visit coffee shops off campus? Since this will not be the last coffee talk you have, it would benefit you greatly to check out the local eateries and coffee shops a bit more thoroughly. This will help you perform at your best because you'll feel at ease when meeting up with your contact.

It's very difficult to be yourself and to have a great conversation in an unfamiliar environment. If you feel uneasy about the coffee shop or unsure about the area, it will negatively affect your conversation. While it may seem like a small detail, practicing the law of familiarity helps you focus on your guest and on the details of the conversation, as opposed to all the other minute details surrounding your meeting. Decide in advance what you'll order to eat or drink and scope out the layout of the eatery beforehand so the only thing you have to focus on is making a great connection over conversation.

2. The power of rehearsal

In each of your coffee talks, the conversation will include a few critical pieces of information. By rehearsing the answers to some common questions, you'll be prepared with clear and definitive talking points when the time comes. An answer delivered with clarity instead of hesitation can make all the difference in how you present yourself.

It's normal to feel a bit nervous and unsure during a coffee talk. Another purpose for rehearsing some of your responses is to boost your confidence. Practicing rehearsed answers before a coffee talk makes us more comfortable and less nervous in conversation. Before a coffee talk, prepare answers to the following prompts and then rehearse them out loud:

1) *Tell me about yourself.*

2) *Where do you see yourself in the next three to five years?*

3) *What kind of work experience do you have?*

4) *What are your professional interests?*

5) *What questions do you have for me?*

6) *How can I help you?*

3. Early arrival

To be early is to be on time, to be on time is to be late, and to be late is to be forgotten. I can't stress this point enough. Arriving late to a scheduled meet-up is nearly impossible to overcome. It is an unwritten rule for employers never to hire a job candidate who arrives late for an interview. While a coffee meet-up isn't a job interview, it should be treated no differently. Showing up late sends two messages: "This is not important to me" and "I don't respect your time." Don't be late!

To ensure this never happens to you, make it a priority to arrive at least fifteen minutes early to any appointment you schedule. If you're scheduled to meet at noon, make a habit of showing up at 11:45. An early arrival gives you several advantages. For one, it gives you the opportunity to gather your thoughts so that you don't feel rushed into conversation. It also gives your contact the impression that you are a punctual person. As a result, your contact will naturally associate you with other positive qualities: competence, intelligence, thoughtfulness, and so on. Start your conversation—and your relationship—on the right foot with an early arrival.

4. The sandwich theory

In her book *The Fine Art of Small Talk,* Debra Fine uses the analogy of a sandwich to describe the perfect conversation. A sandwich has three layers: the top piece of bread (the beginning), the meat and/or other ingredients (the middle), and the bottom piece of bread (the end). Having an understanding of the flow of conversation can drastically improve your conversational skills. Here are some more details about the layers:

- **The top piece of bread: Small talk.** The typical networking conversation almost always begins with small talk. For a few minutes, the two parties will warm up to each other by covering topics such as the weather, a recent sporting event, or some good news that they recently received. Small talk is your icebreaker. This top layer of bread cannot be overlooked when it comes to networking in one-on-one scenarios. It may be "small," but it's essential. In fact, skilled small talk generally leads to great big talk. The better you do it, the better your chances of making a seamless transition to the meat of the conversation.

- **The meat/substance.** After the small talk comes the big talk. It's the reason why the conversation is taking place. It's the part of the conversation when the most valuable information is exchanged. This is the section of the coffee talk when you can expect to receive some variation of the six questions for which you have prepared and rehearsed. In the process, your contact will probably give you information about his or her job/company/industry, background, and advice about approaching the job-hunting process while in college. (If your contact *doesn't* share this kind of information, it's your responsibility to request it.)

- **The bottom piece of bread: the closure.** After an exchange of industry information, personal anecdotes, and potential ways to help you (remember, this is why you are meeting!), the coffee talk will come to a brief but ever-so-important close. How you part is just as important, if not more so, than how you began. The best conversations end on a light note, no matter the circumstance. Skilled networkers close out coffee talks just as they started—with lighthearted, pleasurable conversation. Find a way to leave the conversation on a high note and with a smile.

5. Identify calls to action (CTAs)

To seal the deal in a coffee talk, the last step is to identify your calls to action (CTAs). After the conversation, who is going to follow up? By when? What did you agree upon as the next step, and how will this next step be taken?

If you want your coffee talks to turn into immediate action, you can't afford to overlook this step. Most college students leave the task of identifying CTAs for an ambiguous time in the future. Don't do this! Details get lost in translation quickly. Time passes, and the next thing you know, it's been two months and you haven't gotten in touch with your contact since your coffee talk. Remember, this responsibility is on your shoulders, not theirs.

Identifying your CTAs *immediately* after the conclusion of the coffee talk puts positive pressure on both you and your contact to get things moving to help you. Additionally, people think highly of those who are organized and who keep them accountable. Adopt the habit of identifying actionable steps as soon as possible—it will help you produce the desired results from your coffee talks.

Chapter Takeaways

- A first impression can make all the difference when you're networking. Gather the five ingredients to a great first impression:

  - Dress to impress

  - Smile first

  - Be expectant

  - Use positive body language

  - Use intriguing, open-ended questions

- An informational interview gives you the chance to learn about any position, company, or industry straight from the horse's mouth. Use the five rungs of research to prepare for these invaluable interviews with working professionals.

- The coffee talk is a fundamental aspect of networking in college. It gives you practice for the real world after graduation. Follow these five steps of preparation to ensure you ace your coffee talk:

  - The law of familiarity

  - The power of rehearsal

  - Punctuality

  - The sandwich theory

  - Identifying calls to action (CTAs)

Calls to Action

- Spend an afternoon identifying two off-campus locations that you will use for future coffee talks. Find out their prices, best drinks and dishes, and open hours.

- Using the most successful person you know personally, answer the following questions: How does this person dress? How often does he or she smile in conversation? How well does he or she carry a conversation? What kinds of questions does he or she ask? How would you describe his or her body language?

- *Never* enter a job interview blind! Use the informational interview technique to speak with someone who knows about the industry, the organization, or the position itself in detail.

- Always use the five rungs of research to help you prepare for an informational interview.

- Use the five ingredients of a great first impression to meet one new person routinely (one per week, one per month, etc.). Take note of what works for you and how you can alter your approach. This is how you network!

6 THINK BIG(GER)

*Not many people believe that they can move mountains so as a
result, not many do.*

—David J. Schwartz, *The Magic of Thinking Big*

If you could get in touch with only one person in the
entire world, who would it be? What is the most important
issue you'd love to help solve in a particular industry? Nine
out of ten people will never take the jump to act on their
answers to these questions, let alone to jot down their
answers. Before we begin, the rational part of our brain
jumps in and tells us all the reasons why we should refrain
from answering questions we couldn't possibly act on.

It never crossed my mind to think about these kinds of
questions until I came across *The Magic of Thinking Big*, a
book written by David Schwartz in 1959. The concepts that
Schwartz presents are simple, effective, and undoubtedly
timeless—the book has sold over four million copies since

its publication. Here are ten of the book's ideas that stuck with me:

1. "Think success all the time, never failure."

2. "Never underestimate your own intelligence. Never overestimate the intelligence of others."

3. "Never regret your actions."

4. "Action always cures fear."

5. "People are far more alike than they are different."

6. "It's okay to fail. It's not okay to not try."

7. "You're better than you think you are."

8. "Continue to stretch your vision."

9. "Don't let tradition paralyze your mind."

10. "Do things for the right reasons."

When you apply these maxims to networking, your ideas about what is and isn't possible for you begin to change. You begin to view taking risks not as a liability but as a necessary part of success. *There is no better time than your college years to think big.* There will never again come a time in your life when it is better to assume risk than right now. Your responsibilities are few, and your resources are virtually unlimited. Think of it this way: failing to take chances on the great opportunities available to you during college could be considered tuition money gone down the drain.

Risk taking looks different for everyone. But when you apply Schwartz's ten simple concepts and begin to *think big*, I can promise you that you will see opportunities you never saw before. You will turn into a more creative, opportunistic person, and it will eventually show in how you choose to build new relationships.

The following is an article I wrote in 2014. It's my own networking story, which came as a result of *thinking big*. Let it serve as your inspiration to define your own big, bold, lofty goal and then to go after it with all you've got. What do you have to lose?

Networking comes in a variety of shapes, forms, and sizes. While it can be extremely valuable to build relationships with peers and colleagues, wouldn't it be amazing to quantum leap to the top and connect directly with industry-shaping juggernauts? Whether you are proposing a bold business plan or seeking simple advice, getting through to these pioneers is no simple task—particularly for those of us who are just starting out.

The first-year analyst. The unpaid intern. Even the ambitious college student. We all wrestle with the same daunting question: how does the little guy network with the really, really big guy?

Most people are taken aback when they hear about the people I have been able to reach, especially when I reveal that at the time I was a recent college graduate with less than one year of work experience. This past year, one of these "unreachables" I had the fortune of connecting with was John Bogle.

An acclaimed member of the 2004 TIME 100 Most Influential People in the World list, Jack Bogle revolutionized investing when he introduced low-cost index funds to the financial market. He is the founder and retired CEO of the Vanguard Group, one of the world's largest investment companies, with over three trillion dollars in assets under management. I'd like to add that Mr. Bogle is an absolute gentleman. I'll forever remain grateful for his lending time and wisdom that changed my way of thinking and opened doors I never would have attempted to step through had we not conversed.

How did *I* do it? My resume is no more impressive than the next college graduate's. At the time of our conversation, I had not one referral that could put me in touch with the finance guru. So, what did it? In short, it was my realization that while we cannot spontaneously create years of work experience, we can certainly create value. By following the three Be's, you can find yourself sharing ideas and developing relationships with the unreachables, or whomever you choose to reach: Be bold. Be visible. Be valuable.

Here are the four networking tips that helped me secure a thirty-five-minute phone call with one of the greatest financial investors of the twentieth century.

1. Big (Well-Thought-Out!) Ideas Attract Big People

If at first the idea is not absurd, then there is no hope for it.
—Albert Einstein

Should student-athletes be paid? If so, how would it work?

I had just entered the world of college athletics as a first-year administrator. Conceptualizing a blueprint for a potential multibillion-dollar business solution wasn't exactly in my job description, nor was it the common weekend activity for a recent college grad. But as a young professional, I wanted to test the boundaries. I knew that in order to network effectively and impressively, I had to make up in **value** and innovation what I lacked in experience. When I began to share The SARA (student athlete retirement arrangement) Initiative within my circle of friends, they both challenged and lauded my model for its daringness.

I took action on my bold idea. It became my main talking point when speaking with others. Eventually, I mustered up the confidence to reach out to Mr. Bogle's office for both strategic advice and possible support in my efforts. He got word of the concept, applauded the innovative thinking, and agreed to a scheduled phone call with me. (Note: When Jack introduced the low-cost index fund to the market, it was an idea both challenged and lauded for its daringness.)

So, what's the lesson to be learned? Am I an undercover business genius oozing with the solutions to all problems? Not in the least. The truth of the matter is that big, well-thought-out ideas are tangible forces that *move* people. There is power in thinking big and following through on it. Ideas with the potential to create seismic value have a knack for attracting big people, regardless of whether they come from a senior executive or a college student.

Your big, well-thought-out idea may or may not be accepted. This doesn't really matter. What does matter is that you've created potential value that has given you the opportunity to become **visible** and to partake in a discussion that you otherwise would have no business being a part of. Put in the work to create your big ideas and allow them to attract you to big people. What's the worst that could happen? You get no response. The best? You land a one-on-one meeting and an incredible opportunity to connect with someone like Jack Bogle.

Ask yourself these three questions when starting out:

1. What is the single most prevalent and potentially devastating issue facing my company and/or industry?

2. If I were responsible for solving this issue, what would be my solution?

3. What person in my company/industry would find this information useful?

2. Persistence Is Everything

Success seems to be largely a matter of hanging on after others have let go. —William Feather

From the day I reached out to Jack's office to the day I got through, nearly four months had passed. My first cold e-mail remained unanswered after a few weeks, so I sent a gentle reminder asking for a very brief, ten-minute phone call to solicit advice about my proposed solution, which I had derived from the answers to the three questions above. (Note: Always ask for a specific amount of time, preferably less time than you need.) I finally received an e-mail stating that I should send another e-mail in a month's time to check in when Mr. Bogle's schedule was less busy. This exchange continued for some time.

While making repetitive phone calls and sending reminder e-mails isn't the most glamorous way to spend your time, you must understand that unreachables are incredibly busy—hence the nickname. Your inquiries rank last on their priority list. This is where the personal growth for you happens. Stick with it and remain positive.

As in my case, it may take weeks or even months to reach an unreachable. But with persistence, you will have your sliver of opportunity, during which you must present yourself as someone worth the time of day. But not to worry, you've prepared for this moment, and you were made to impress. You're more than ready.

3. Know Your Purpose and Stick to It

Simplicity is the ultimate form of sophistication. —Leonardo da Vinci

Why am I reaching out? What is my purpose? What is my motive?

Following tips 1 and 2 will prepare you to answer these questions. Oftentimes, young professionals try to network with no pointed purpose. They don't know *why* they wish to connect; instead, they believe that brushing shoulders with someone of importance will pay off in some arbitrary way. If you were a CEO or president—or anyone who values his or her time—would you give your time to a stranger who has asked no pointed questions and has suggested no clear purpose for a conversation? It's highly doubtful.

Keep your reasons for reaching out painfully simple and honest. It will cut down the time that an unreachable has to spend deciphering what he or she can help you with, thus giving you a better chance to make that connection.

4. Humility and Assertiveness: Find the Happy Medium

It's perfectly fine to be confident in your work. You've put in an incredible amount of time to prepare yourself for this once-in-a-lifetime networking opportunity. But please keep in mind that the unreachable may have amassed as many years in his or her industry as you have had on this earth. Use the following points to help you find the happy medium between displaying humility and asserting yourself as a worthy networker:

- If the unreachable has written a book, read the book. (Bogle's *Little Book of Common Sense Investing* was a great read.)

- If the unreachable has any videos, recent interviews, or speeches available online, watch them. (You get the pattern here?)

Without being prompted, make it clear that you have done your due diligence and that you are well versed with regards to your unreachable's work and accomplishments.

In these circumstances, failing to prepare is truly preparing to fail. Being prepared is not as much flattery as it is following the hidden code of ethics for networking.

My phone call with Mr. Bogle changed the trajectory of my entire year for the better. It opened the doors for amazing opportunities, provided me the chance to meet incredible people, and, above all, gave me the confidence to network with just about anyone. Don't be afraid to go for it! Use these four networking tips to be bold, to be visible, and to be valuable. Happy networking.

When looking back at this period in my early professional life, I have absolutely no regrets. The one lesson I learned—and the lesson I hope you takeaway— is that most of us create imaginary ceilings when we think of what is possible for us. When you combine the skillset of networking with ability to think big, you will undoubtedly surprise yourself with what you believe is possible. And once you change your belief about what is possible, the actions you take will reflect that change. Use my story as well as my experience to aid you in thinking creatively about how to take action on your big idea. Never be afraid to think outside of the box and always think big!

Chapter Takeaways

- Limited thinking brings limited results. Don't be afraid to think big(ger) when networking. You've got nothing to lose.

- Remember these four tips when you make your attempt to network with the big dogs:

  - Big, well-thought-out ideas attract big people.

  - Persistence is everything.

  - Know your purpose and stick to it.

  - Find the balance between assertiveness and humility.

Calls to Action

- If you knew you could not fail, what big, bold idea, project, or initiatives would you pursue? Try to list ten ideas, and choose the best one. Try this exercise with a friend.

- What one person is a household name in your desired industry? What are three ways you could attempt to get in touch with this individual? Now, do it! Think creatively, and be persistent.

- If you could speak with this person for just ten minutes, what is the one thing you'd want to learn? What is the one thing you would want to make sure he or she knows about you?

- Think back to the boldest thing you've ever accomplished in your life. What mental obstacles did you overcome to accomplish the feat? How did the accomplishment make you feel?

SECTION III.
THE OUTREACH

7 ON-CAMPUS NETWORKING

The world is our university and everyone you encounter is your teacher. When you wake up each day, make sure you go to school.

—T. D. Jakes, author of *Instinct*

Invite people into your life who don't look like you; don't think like you; don't act like you, don't come from where you come from—and you might find that they will challenge your assumptions and make you grow as a person.

—Mellody Hobson, president, Ariel Investments

What's Your Networking Plan?

When he took his first step on the campus of Florida State University, Myron Rolle had a networking plan for his success. Rolle was a gifted student and an exceptional athlete in college, but what strikes me most was Rolle's ability to build a network that supported his lofty goals during his time at Florida State. The following is an excerpt from Myron's opening statement before the Senate Commerce, Science, and Transportation Committee hearing on College Athletes and Academics on July 9, 2014.

> *I decided to go to Florida State. When I got to Tallahassee on campus, [the] first thing I did was go to the office of national fellowships and tell them that I wanted to be a Rhodes Scholar like my hero Bill Bradley. If he did it, I wanted to try and do it as well. And so three years later, I was fortunate enough to earn that scholarship. Then I went to see my teachers and academic advisors at FSU, and tell them that I want you [guys] to help increase my intellectual capital so one day I can be an outstanding pediatric neurosurgeon like another one of my influences, Dr. Ben Carson. Now I'm a second-year medical student, hopefully able to do that in the future. Lastly, I went to my strength coaches, my athletic trainers, and my football coaches, Bobby Bowden included, and told them that I want[ed] them to equip my body and get me ready for a career as a national football player. Fortunately I was able to be drafted by the Titans and play for the Steelers as well.*

It was evident that Myron Rolle instinctively knew the importance of building a network in college. More important, with amazing accomplishment after amazing accomplishment, Rolle's story illustrates to us all the power of having a networking plan, and how this plan can help aid us in achieving our goals—however lofty our goals may be.

The Strength of Weak Ties

The year 1973 marked the publication of Stanford sociologist Mark Granovetter's *The Strength of Weak Ties*, one of the most influential studies on networking ever published. In the study, Granovetter analyzed strong ties and weak ties and the various ways in which our networks influence the job opportunities that come our way. He defined a strong tie as a connection to a close friend—someone with whom we are well acquainted. A weak tie, as you may guess, can be defined as a distant acquaintance. Weak ties are connections to individuals who travel in different social circles yet remain tangentially connected to us. The study revealed that contrary to popular belief, job opportunities are considerably more likely to come from our weak ties than our strong ones. This is largely because our strong ties rarely provide us with information we do not already know. On the other hand, because they do not frequent the same social circles, weak ties provide us with new opportunities and new information that can benefit us tremendously. Granovetter's work empirically proved that networking helps people land the jobs of their dreams.

For the purposes of networking, here is the bottom line of Granovetter's groundbreaking study: if you want more (and better) exposure to job opportunities, you need more weak-tie relationships in your network. Weak ties are your links to new worlds. They broaden your horizons and expose you to opportunities you would miss out on otherwise. So, here's the question: what do these weak ties look like in college, and how do you go about forming them?

In this chapter we will focus on three areas that will help strengthen your weak ties on campus: social comfort zones, student organizations, and student-professor relationships.

Social Comfort Zones

A comfort zone is a beautiful place. But nothing ever grows there. —Unknown

If you can begin to understand how your social circles define most of your relationships, you can then see in plain sight the steps you will need to take to find and strengthen invaluable weak ties. Your social circles reveal a great deal about you. Where you spend your time, whom you interact with, and where your interests lie are by-products of your social circles. You can identify weak-tie relationships by counting the number of mutual friends between you and another individual. The lower the number of mutual friends you have, the weaker the tie.

Now, how can you define your social circles so that you know when you are creating weak ties as opposed to strong ones? Here's a helpful exercise. In a Profound Ivy spring workshop, I asked students to draw a Venn diagram of the three social circles with which they most identified on campus. To complete the exercise, each student wrote down all of his weekly activities and then condensed the list into three overarching categories—sports, activity clubs, student organizations, and so on.

We highlighted one student as an example. He was a senior with just a month and a half left in his college career.

We categorized his activities into three social circles: Football, Eating Club, and Bible study group. (An eating club is very much what it sounds like. Think of a dining hall/social house hybrid, to which a select group of people belongs.) After breaking down his weekly activities across the entire campus, he was certain that over the past three and a half years, he had spent at least 90 percent of his time with people who were involved in those three social circles. While I'm sure he built some tremendous friendships within these circles, Granovetter tells us that it's the weak ties—the relationships just beyond his social circles, just beyond his comfort zones—that would benefit him most in strengthening his network.

Take the time to try this activity for yourself. Divide your social life into three categories, as I did with Profound Ivy students. Next, brainstorm to identify a person, an activity, or a social event that does *not* fall within your social comfort zone. Then use this information to create an "uncomfortable zone" schedule for yourself. Just once a month, reach out to arrange a lunch with someone you normally wouldn't see on a day-to-day basis. If you enjoy hip-hop music, find a friend who loves classical music and arrange to attend a concert together. If you attend athletic events regularly, switch it up and attend a theater performance. Stick around after it's over, and aim to meet one new person at the event.

These suggestions may sound trivial, but the results are anything but. This is how you begin to build your network. If you create a schedule that disrupts your normal social routine in college, even if only once a month, your weak ties will begin to increase. It takes a fairly low investment, and the exposure to new people and new surroundings opens the door for you to grow both personally and professionally. Play around with your "uncomfortable zone" schedule and see how it works for you.

Industry-Related Student Organizations

So, you're back on campus after the summer, and you have some very specific goals for the year. The first goal you have in mind is to make new friends. Your second goal is to become more active on campus. Your third goal is directly related to gaining more job prospects: you feel like your resume isn't compelling enough, so you want to find long-term activities that will help bring your resume to life and provide you with compelling talking points come interview time.

By joining the right student organization, you can knock out three birds with one stone.

It goes without saying that your time in college is valuable. When you invest considerable time and effort into any particular activity or organization, you want to ensure you get in return what I like to call unusual value. This is what one of my Profound Ivy mentees did, and it worked out for him in a great way. For the sake of anonymity, let's call him Terry.

Terry was looking to network in the sports management industry, but he was having a difficult time finding mentors, contacts, and available internships for the upcoming summer. In the spring of his junior year,

110

Terry decided to join an existing on-campus student group for students interested in the sports industry. The organization had only a handful of active members, very little organization, and dwindling participation over the course of the year. Terry recruited a few friends and took action to revamp the student group. With the help of financial backing from the school (virtually all colleges are mandated to create a budget for student-led organizations, especially organizations with concrete plans for using the money), Terry was rewarded for his efforts. The small group took an hour-long train ride into the metropolitan area to attend the New York City conference, where Terry connected with dozens of sports industry professionals. It didn't hurt that he was a key organizer of the trip! Terry returned to campus with three interviews lined up in the following three weeks.

The interviews that practically landed in Terry's lap are the same interviews that students across the country were applying for online, as they crossed their fingers and desperately hoped for some kind of response at some point in the future. By acting on his instincts, Terry bypassed the cold resume stage and replaced it with an in-person handshake and a smile.

Joining a student organization that is related to your desired future work or industry is one of the easiest ways to attract great opportunities for the future. For one, it keeps you active in the industry by giving you the chance to attend events, lectures, and discussion groups that keep you informed and up-to-date with the ever-changing aspects of that specific work community. Second, you can make friends with students who have similar career goals. You can learn from each other, challenge each other, and support each other whenever things get difficult. These kinds of relationships are irreplaceable.

Relationships with Professors: How to Break the Barrier

For many students, the way in which they experienced school for the first eighteen years of their lives led them to view a classroom as a scene of student versus instructor. Then, in college, instead of viewing their professors as the incredible resources that they are, these students see professors as their nemeses, intent on keeping everyone from succeeding in the classroom. For this reason and others, students are hesitant to cross the line between students and professors. This kind of thinking prevents the large majority of students from building healthy student-professor relationships and experiencing all the tremendous advantages that come with them.

I learned the hard way that a good relationship with a professor can make all the difference. As a college student-athlete, you can expect that you'll be forced to miss a chunk of classes, to ask for makeup test dates, and to petition for multiple deadline extensions. It comes with the territory. When you're traveling across the country for intercollegiate competition, your schedule can become overwhelming. Student-professor relationships must be strong for a student to combat these outside factors.

Over time, I realized that the better my communication and transparency with my professors, the better the relationship—and the better the relationship, the better I performed in the classroom. When I took the preliminary step of scheduling in-person discussions with professors about my upcoming football, basketball, or track and field schedule, I gained the kind of trust and respect that extended well beyond the classroom. On the other hand, when I didn't proactively take this step, my professors couldn't have cared less about helping me work around my schedule conflicts. Whether or not I succeeded academically was heavily dependent upon how well I crossed the student-professor barrier.

So, what is this barrier I speak of? It's the invisible-but-ever-so-present force field that separates the student and the professor. To many, professors can seem both unapproachable and even intimidating at times. For this reason, most college students don't prioritize befriending their professors. I, however, quickly learned an unforgettable lesson: it is *always* good practice to create a transparent relationship with people who are responsible for evaluating your performance (professors, bosses, and so on). For one, an established relationship helps give you a clear picture of what is expected of you, and thus a better chance to perform at a high level. Two, it earns you the benefit of the doubt when things go awry. And as any seasoned college student would tell you, at some point in time things will go awry.

Breaking the barrier is a strategy that I learned through personal experience. I've seen Profound Ivy mentees put this practice into effect and improve their academic performance. This strategy is incredibly easy to understand but not always easy to apply. However, building a rapport with your professors can be one of the best investments you ever make in your college experience. Professors are some of the best-connected, most resourceful individuals on campus, and they can even serve as incredible mentors. Given the hundreds—sometimes thousands—of students they've shepherded through the university gates, you can bet they've heard your story before. With that kind of wisdom in your vicinity, it'd be unfortunate not to see if you can learn a thing or two outside the lecture hall.

Here are four steps you can take to break the barrier and to create more personal relationships with your professors.

1) The power of the personal introduction

The number one reason why a personal introduction is incredibly effective in breaking the barrier and developing a healthy rapport with your professors is that *98 percent of students do not do it*. The vast majority of your peers will not proactively introduce themselves to their professors. Those who do are almost always the students who find ways to get the most out of their experiences and perform tremendously in the class. The first step you can take to build the foundation for a great relationship is simply to introduce yourself. Insist on a meeting. Stop by *before* the semester begins so that both of you can put a face with a name, and express your excitement about taking this professor's course because (insert well-crafted, thoughtful answer here).

The more often you engage your professor in a one-on-one scenario, the greater the chance of breaking the barrier and establishing a relationship that can benefit you long after the grades are in and the semester is over. Use the e-mail template below to request a brief meeting with your professors prior to the beginning of the semester.

Dear Professor _____,

I hope this e-mail finds you well. My name is _____, and I will be taking your course _____ this fall. I know your schedule is busy, but I would love to stop by your office for five minutes this week to introduce myself. Can you please let me know a convenient time?

I am very much looking forward to the semester!

All the best,

_____

If you can look over the syllabus and find one or two questions that you'd like to discuss, be sure to do so. If your professor has recently written an article or been interviewed about a topic that interests you, reach out and let him or her know you'd love to discuss the topic in greater detail.

2) The power of office hours

One of the most common misconceptions that can cripple college students is the idea that they should seek out campus resources only when their academic performance is poor. For example, they find the tutor *after* they receive the first D on a midterm exam. They join a study group *after* their GPA drops to an unacceptable level. Many students see office hours as a last resort—as a lifeline rather than the consistent support system that they really are.

Change your thinking as follows: "Office hours are my best friend. They allow me to build great relationships with my professors." In college I was taken aback when I realized that some of the best-performing students attended open office hours routinely. After all of their questions were answered, they often stuck around to chat with the professor as well as the preceptors. Why? Because they knew all too well what it takes to break the barrier.

If you want to build a relationship with your professor, show up to office hours. You'll find that professors are people—usually incredibly interesting people—and if you show their class enough respect, they will be more than happy to return the favor. Attending office hours is a great way of keeping open a line of communication that can return to you tremendous value in both the short-term and the long-term future.

3) The power of vulnerability

As a premedical student in my sophomore year, I had several questions about my career path. I had lingering doubts as to whether a medical career was right for me. Did I want to continue on this path? Did I *really* love medicine enough to commit the next six years to school? I found these tough, personal questions difficult to discuss with others. Running out of ideas, I turned to my chemistry professor, to whom I was not particularly close before our conversation. I asked him if we could sit down and talk. I wanted his advice on my situation and his thoughts about sticking with medicine or changing my major completely.

I was confused and vulnerable. Here I was, a nineteen-year-old kid asking for some real advice. I didn't know what to do. In our conversation, through his careful answers and empathetic approach, I realized that we were breaking a barrier. No longer was a professor speaking to a student. Now, a man thirty years my senior was empathizing with a young man wrestling with difficult life choices. As we spoke, I could feel the barrier melting between us. He became a trusted source and an investor in my well-being as well as my future. He told me time and time again that he wanted nothing more than to see me succeed.

I leaned on that relationship for the remainder of my time at Princeton. Even when I decided to depart from the premed route, I continued to check in every now and then and to bounce ideas off of him. Opening up to my professor was difficult, but in the process I created a strong bond that became invaluable to me.

I learned an incredibly valuable lesson from my experience, and that lesson was this: there is tremendous networking power *even* in our vulnerability. Don't limit the relationship-building process to the high points of your life. People who have the courage to ask for advice have the power to create *real* bonds. As a student, this lesson is gold. If you can muster the courage never to tackle difficult situations alone, and if you take a chance and allow a professor to help you with a tough predicament or decision, you'll find that professors—and individuals all across campus—are there to help you through almost anything. You will go through tough times and tough decisions in college, as everyone will. What distinguishes you is how you handle these difficulties.

Ask your professors for real-world advice! Their wealth of knowledge may surprise you.

4) Millionaire's row

Sitting in the front row of the class, also known as millionaire's row, puts you in prime position to stand out and to break the barrier with your professors. Students who sit in the front row commonly develop the following habits: they dress appropriately for class, they are punctual, they ask questions regularly, they attend office hours, and they retain more of the lecture's information.

At seminars and professional conferences, people have nicknamed the front row "millionaire's row" for the simple reason that it represents the doers, the go-getters, the action-oriented people. When you sit in the front row, you signal to the lecturer, "I'm here to learn." It's also a physical reminder that all of your attention needs to be directly on the lecturer, because that's why you're there. Finally, it transforms you from a face in the sea to a recognizable, active, and engaged student. It is much easier to begin a relationship with a professor on the right foot when you're the student who sits front and center at every lecture.

When building your network in college, it's important that you start on campus by forging incredible weak-tie relationships—relationships that connect you with individuals and opportunities that normally would lie well beyond the scope of your everyday social interactions. Identify your social comfort zone and build a schedule to periodically take a step outside of it. Join a career-oriented, on-campus student organization that can put you in the right circles and keep you learning more about your industry. Finally, befriend your professors. Follow the four-step process that will help you break the usual student-professor barrier and experience college in a more personal, quality manner.

Chapter Takeaways

- Building an on-campus network is a proven method for succeeding in college.

- Weak-tie relationships are powerful. They bring you more opportunities and add incredible value to your network.

- There are numerous advantages to building relationships with your college professors. Follow the four-step process to break the barrier and to take advantage of these great relationships.

Calls to Action

- Take a blank sheet of paper and jot down the three social groups/locations on campus that occupy the majority of your time in college.

- Create an "uncomfortable zone" schedule to build weak-tie relationships that belong in a fourth social group. This schedule can include attending a new event on campus or grabbing lunch with someone you rarely spend time with. Think creatively.

- Schedule an in-person meeting with each of your professors prior to the beginning of each semester.

- Join a student organization that is related to your desired work industry. If none exists, find people with similar interests, and create one!

8 OFF-CAMPUS NETWORKING

The best time to plant a tree was twenty years ago.
The next best time is today.

—Chinese proverb

To those who know the place well, Princeton University is commonly referred to as the Orange Bubble. The small township of Princeton is tucked into the center of the state of New Jersey. At the heart of the township you'll find the university, surrounded by greenery and suburbia that stretches for miles in every direction. The campus is heavily insulated, a fact that can be considered both an advantage and a disadvantage when it comes to building a network in college.

The bubble effect at a place like Princeton is fairly common on college campuses. Universities across the country buzz with so many concurrent activities that it's easy for students to lose sight of anything that's happening off campus. You can easily spend four (or more) years with on-campus tunnel vision and fail to build contacts outside of the bubble. In the previous chapter, we discussed weak-tie relationships and the strategies you can use to network on campus. The question for this chapter is, how do you balance your on-campus network by building a sustainable network off campus as well? To ensure that you maintain your networking equilibrium, you must tap into something called networking ecosystems.

What Is a Networking Ecosystem?

A networking ecosystem is comprised of a group of people who share a common experience and/or interest and join together for the purpose of professional advancement. These groups provide assistance to each other via career advice, personal and professional referrals, internships, and even full-time jobs.

Networking ecosystems can help diversify your social groups as well as your experiences, thus leading to a broader scope of opportunities. They can also prevent you from becoming a homebody "bubble dependent" on campus who relies solely on campus relationships to experience college.

A networking ecosystem ensures that you are building a network, not just a community. What's the difference? A community is something you belong to; a network is something that belongs to you. To build these networks and to transcend your college community, commit yourself to stepping out of your comfort zone, rolling up your sleeves, and tapping in to the opportunities that await your arrival.

As you may guess, it's imperative not only to join multiple networking ecosystems, but also to become actively involved in them. In this chapter we'll take an in-depth look at three ecosystems and explore some practical ways in which you could make them work for you while in college.

1) Big-City Conference Events

When in doubt, volunteer it out! All year round, you can find large-scale conferences and events designed to attract working professionals. It is uncommon for students to hear about these opportunities because such events are targeted primarily to individuals who are already well into their working careers. If you approach these conferences and events in the right way, they are networking golden nuggets. From my experience, any event manager would love to have an extra hand who is willing to do dirty work—move chairs, clean up, organize placards, pass out flyers, and so on. While it may not sound like the most appealing way to spend your time, volunteering at these kinds of events is invaluable. It gives you access to a networking ecosystem that can benefit you in multiple ways.

When I worked for the Princeton athletic department, we hosted the ninth annual Ivy Sports Symposium, heralded as one of the global sports industry's premier events. That year's Ivy Sports Symposium had over five hundred attendees and featured ninety-five speakers. In attendance were Major League Baseball team presidents, professional sports team general managers, senior executive sports writers, and many more seasoned professionals. It was heaven for any young guy or gal even somewhat interested in working in the sports industry. In our office at the time, we had a new intern named Mike, who was a junior in college and a sports fanatic. He had heard about the Ivy Sports Symposium and wanted to take full advantage of it.

"Hey, Isaac," he said to me one day, "I think I'm going to try and attend that symposium. Are there any tickets left?"

It's free for college students, so you won't need a ticket," I replied. "But I've got an even better idea for you. You should volunteer. I know we are short on hands right now, and I know they will find some work for you to do. Who knows, you might meet some great people behind the scenes."

Mike took my advice. When the day of the symposium rolled around, I showed up at the event to receive my name tag.

"Here's your name tag, Isaac," I heard a man say.

It was Mike, dressed in his finest suit and the brightest smile I'd ever seen from him.

"They placed me at the sign-in table, and I get the chance to meet almost every attendee personally," Mike reported. "I've already scheduled a few phone calls with some heavy hitters! Thanks for the advice, man."

By volunteering rather than just attending, Mike leveraged his seemingly menial position as the "name tag guy" to interact with more people than probably any other attendee at the entire conference. In other words, he hustled.

Be like Mike! See the opportunity disguised behind every opportunity. Go the extra mile by volunteering at events. It almost always returns extraordinary results.

Don't forget about the event organizers!

It's always a fantastic experience for a college kid to schmooze with the big names. At the same time, never lose sight of the people who gave you the opportunity in the first place. Coordinators and event managers of large conferences are some of the best-connected individuals you will ever meet. If you do a great job with every task that is assigned to you; if you make it a priority to show up early and never leave without asking how else you can be of assistance; and if you follow up and thank the person who granted you the opportunity to volunteer, you will have built a strong reputation within a new networking ecosystem. In many cases, it's the coordinators and managers behind the scenes who will help you out the most. Do a terrific job as a volunteer, and watch as opportunities begin to make themselves available to you via your new networking ecosystem.

2) Career Services Center

Although your college career services center is technically an on-campus ecosystem, most of the center's contacts are off-campus, across the country and even span the globe. The career services center serves as a terrific networking ecosystem because company recruiters, employers, and working professionals make a beeline to this office when they want to reach out to college students. Without a doubt, career services centers are some of the least utilized resources on college campuses. Students often go there as a last resort when the job hunt is too much to bear alone. In a best-case scenario, students should routinely check in with career services throughout the course of the semester.

Creating a long-term relationship with your career services center is a great way to tap into a highly valuable networking ecosystem. Attend sponsored events, and volunteer if you can. In doing so, you'll surround yourself with professionals whose job is to help you solidify your postgraduate plans. In addition, you'll be the first to know when companies and employers that interest you will be on campus.

Just as you meet your professors at the beginning of each semester, carve out time at the start of each academic year to talk with staff members at career services and to attend one of the center's events. When you talk with folks there, be direct about the kinds of opportunities you are looking for, and ask about the best ways to find and to prepare for these opportunities. With regards to seeking employment and creating job prospects, there may not be a more easily accessible resource to you than the career services networking ecosystem.

3) High School

This is one networking ecosystem that many college students discount time and time again. You're probably thinking, "How can my high school community help me?" When you were a high school student, you probably didn't view your surroundings as a valuable employment resource, but that was only because you were a high school student. Now you're in college, and your needs have evolved. You can see your past from a different vantage point.

Your high school network is likely the largest social network you have back in your hometown. Fellow alumni/ae, old high school friends, coaches, teachers, and administrators can all become great resources for you if you approach them in the right way.

So, how do you tap in to this networking ecosystem? First, find out if your high school has already established a career and networking group. If there is an alumni newsletter, review it for career-related events and opportunities. You might be surprised to know how many high schools have well-organized alumni organizations that would be glad to involve young alumni like you.

Don't allow your high school contacts to grow stale as you grow comfortable in the college world. Reach back and remain in touch. This way, if you ever go home for winter and summer breaks, or even for postgraduation life, you'll have a starting point from which to network and to seek out opportunities.

Chapter Takeaways

- Becoming too immersed in the college bubble can be detrimental to your personal and professional development.

- Join off-campus networking ecosystems to give your network balance.

- Tap into the power of volunteering to extend the reach of your network.

Calls to Action

- Using your college's career services center, identify at least two large-scale local conferences for which you could volunteer. These can be general conferences (such as TED Talks) or industry-specific ones (such as a sports professionals conference).

- Early on in the academic year, schedule a one-on-one meeting with a representative of your career services center. Lay out your interests, passions, and professional goals with this person's assistance so that he or she can help you identify promising opportunities. Ask for assistance in identifying key career-planning information—application deadlines, key alumni/ae in your desired industry, and upcoming on-campus events related to your career interests.

- Sign up for your high school newsletter, and stay on the lookout for opportunities in your hometown. Volunteer for alumni-related tasks whenever you can. Don't let your relationship with your high school community fade away!

.

9 THE POWER OF MENTORSHIP

Show me a successful individual and I'll show you someone who had real positive influences in his or her life. I don't care what you do for a living—if you do it well I'm sure there was someone cheering you on or showing the way. A mentor."

—Denzel Washington

If you dig deep enough, you'll find that behind every success story lie the groundwork and influence of a mentor. Oprah Winfrey looked to Maya Angelou. Denzel Washington had Sidney Poitier. Henry David Thoreau absorbed wisdom from Ralph Waldo Emerson. Even Plato had Socrates. Mentorship has always played a pivotal role in personal growth and maturation. We look to those who have walked the path we wish to take so that we may learn how to dodge some of the potholes they fell into along the way. We look to mentors for guidance, for wisdom, and sometimes just for a listening ear.

Your college years are perhaps the most pivotal time in your life for taking on a mentor. Here you are, standing at the crossroad between adolescence and adulthood, and the decisions you make now are a bit more difficult and far more substantial than they were before. You are exposed to new ideas and situations almost daily, and it's unfair and unrealistic to expect that you'll make all the right decisions on your own. You need mentors—the *right* mentors—in your life.

The Origins of Mentorship

The concept of mentoring can be traced all the way to ancient Greece in Homer's classic poem *The Odyssey*. When Odysseus leaves home to fight in the Trojan War, he leaves behind his infant son Telemachus in the care of a man named Mentor. The war keeps Odysseus away from home for over a decade. In that time, Mentor's responsibility is to fulfill the role of the father: to guide and to "mentor" young Telemachus. Mentor is an educator, guide, trusted adviser, confidant, surrogate parent, and wise and kindly elder. In short, he is whatever Telemachus needs him to be.

The relationship between Mentor and Telemachus gave birth to the concept of mentoring and shaped our view of the modern mentor-mentee relationship. The problem with adopting this viewpoint, however, is that we look for the right mentor instead of the right *mentors*. We expect a parent or someone close to us to provide us with the right kind of support for *all* of our problems, as Mentor does for Telemachus. We run the risk of receiving bad advice from a well-intended person when we look to him or her as an expert on *all* topics instead of the topic for which he or she is best suited.

As comforting as it may be, it's best to resist the temptation of looking to people with whom you are most comfortable for advice that falls outside their expertise. For example, let's say you have a broken bike, and there are two places you can go to get it repaired. The first place is the bike shop way across town. It's a place you rarely visit, but you know that their specialty is fixing bikes. The second option is the corner sandwich shop. Now, the folks at the sandwich shop know nothing about fixing bikes, but they have a few things going for them. For one, you have a tremendous, long-standing relationship with the people at the sandwich shop. Two, you know that they will try to help you fix your bike, regardless of the fact that their specialty is fixing up an incredible roast beef melt. The sandwich shop folks know you and love you. So, where do you go to get your bike fixed? Despite the great sense of comfort between you and the sandwich shop, the bike shop is still the place to go to get expert advice.

Selecting the wrong mentor for the job is just like taking your broken bike to a sandwich shop. You might get some help in the form of moral support, but it won't definitively address your situation. You might laugh at the scenario I've posed, but many of us do this all the time. We look to our parents instead of finding a well-informed professional to help us find a summer internship. We run to listen to people we know rather than sticking our necks out and learning from those we're less familiar with but far better suited to address our dilemma.

To combat this mistake, carefully select your mentors based on who should be diagnosing and helping you address various types of situations in your life. What you're looking for are goal-oriented mentorships.

Goal-Oriented Mentorship

Mentors don't come in one size fits all. On the contrary, a successful mentor-mentee relationship serves a clearly defined purpose and goal. The mentor has a specific role in your life, and *you* define it. In order to follow this model, you'll first need to identify the aspects of your life in which you need help the most. In what specific ways can a mentor help you?

When I decided to write my first book, I knew not one author and had not the slightest clue about the book-publishing process. No one in my family, no friends, and not one colleague had ever written a best-selling book before. I was embarking on a new journey, and I viewed it as my responsibility to go out and find successful authors who had done exactly what I wanted to do. My goal was clear: find successful role models and seek out their mentorship. After doing my research and narrowing my list down to eight successful authors, I began making phone calls, sending e-mails, and organizing coffee talks with these people. Some authors were incredibly accessible; I could find their contact information on the inside flap of their best seller. Others were more difficult to reach. With some authors I had an hour-long conversation over coffee; others answered a single question over e-mail.

Each of these relationships was incredibly important and played a role in my development as an author. Because my goal was specific—and because they had reached the goal themselves—my mentors became heavily invested in seeing me reach it. This process perfectly illustrates how having a desired result in mind will help you identify the best mentors for getting the job done.

So, what are your goals? What are you struggling with? Where do you want to be, and who has already walked the path to that destination? If you are trying to find your way academically, who can mentor you on time management and study tactics? If you want to ace a finance internship interview, who might be able to share his or her mastery of the interview process?

When you use your goals to find the right kind of mentorship, you approach the initial conversation with great purpose, allowing the potential mentor to clearly understand your goal and to help you achieve what you're after. The steps you need to take might not become crystal clear until you sit down, write out your goals, and ask yourself the question, "Who can best help me achieve the right results?" Remember that with every goal you ever set for yourself, there is someone out there who can tell you how to do it.

Career Advice: Alumni Mentorship

One of the best sources for career mentors is your university's alumni/ae database. Once you've identified your career interests, you've got the perfect platform for narrowing down and reaching out to working professionals who have ended up where you hope to be in the future. Your alumni database is a terrific mentor pool for one primary reason. You and every individual in this group already have something in common: a relationship—more than likely a positive one—with your university. This common ground makes for an organic, long-term relationship.

Many university career services offices create alumni databases for the very purpose of mentorship. When I speak on college campuses, I'm amazed at how little students know about the amazing resources that already exist on campus. Use career services as an invaluable resource that connects you with your ideal career mentor.

Academic Support: Peer-to-Peer Mentorship

After I created the Profound Ivy mentorship for Princeton University students, I learned something incredibly eye-opening over the course of two years. When the forty or so student-athletes came together as a community, I realized that each member absorbed information and sustained positive habits best when influenced by their peers. I could lecture all day about the effects of great study habits, but it wasn't until we broke down into subgroups to share knowledge that students began to adapt to their peers and apply what they were learning.

We asked students who performed above average academically to share their study habits and exam-preparation tactics. This activity gave other Profound Ivy students a chance to see classmates achieving the kinds of results they wanted for themselves. It motivated them far more effectively than the suggestions of a professor, a tutor, or me.

Some of your greatest mentors will be your peers, who are there shoulder to shoulder with you. They are people who excel in ways you wish to excel. They are people who find the best ways to study for exams. For whatever reason, it's easy to underestimate how much you can learn from just another college kid. But these are the people who influence your habits, your routines, and your day-to-day life more than anyone else.

Your peers may be the very people who can help you get over the hump. Try something as simple as reaching out to the best performing students in class and asking them about how they study, or finding out if you can join their study group. A step like this can improve your entire academic performance across the board. Many students let their ego get in the way of asking a peer for help. They'd rather trot along, barely keeping their head above water while struggling independently. You might be surprised to discover how many high-achieving students are more than willing to help out.

In my sophomore year, I tried this out myself. I had just received my second C on an exam in a molecular biology class. The next Monday, after class, I approached a student who always arrived early, sat at the front of the room, and actively participated in lecture. I told her how poorly I was doing in the class and asked if she'd mind sharing some study tips. She was more than helpful. She invited me to attend study-group sessions with her and three other students, and I learned that they focused completely on old exams! Each student would take a different old practice exam and grade it, and then the group would walk through each test question by question.

On the next test, I received my first A on a Princeton molecular biology exam, and it was due to the fact that I had put my ego aside and asked my peers to help me.

What's the lesson here? Find students who are performing at a high level, and do exactly as they do. Sometimes it really is as simple as being willing to ask for help.

Become a Mentor

Now you know how to seek out mentorship. You know that it is wise to ask for help. You know that your goals can lead you toward the right kinds of mentors, and you know that your peers can qualify as those mentors. And on top of it all, mentors can serve as a great support staff in your life.

Now it's time to consider returning the favor. Ironically, you can receive just as much as you give when you actively seek out people you can help—when you become a mentor to others.

"But who am I to be a mentor?" This is a common insecurity among college students. Let me remind you that you have excelled in your life—by achieving goals, mastering skill sets, and going to unique places. Other people can benefit tremendously from your experiences, your guidance, and your support.

For example, college students have personal, recent experience with the transition process from high school to college. Many high schools seek college students to mentor their students and to help ease the anxiety surrounding the application process.

To brainstorm other mentorship possibilities, consider these questions:

- What experiences have you had that maybe you have overlooked in the past?

- What are your hobbies?

- What skill sets do you possess?

- What are your natural talents?

Answering these questions will help you carve out what billionaire Warren Buffet calls your "circle of competency." Once you draw this circle, you can feel confident in knowing that there are several ways for you to provide tremendous value as a mentor. You are mentor-worthy, my friend.

Chapter Takeaways

- College is a tough go all by yourself. Find the right mentors to bring perspective, experience, and support to any and all aspects of your life.

- Be careful not to pick the right mentor for the wrong job. Goal-oriented mentorship steers you clear of making this mistake.

- Become a mentor by discovering your "circle of competency" and sharing this competence with those who can benefit.

Calls to Action

- Identify two areas of your life in which you would like to see improvement (time management, academics, athletics, and so on). Do you know people who excel in these areas? Draft an e-mail and set up a conversation with those people specifically to address these issues.

- Identify three personal strengths, talents, and/or skills that make you a potential mentor. Who can best benefit from these assets? Stick to your strengths, and find a way to share your wealth of knowledge.

- Create a schedule with your mentors. Whether it's one phone call per month or a quick e-mail every week, make sure that you have a routine to keep mentors updated on your progress.

10 TIME MANAGEMENT: 10 TIPS FOR SUCCESS

Anything can be accomplished if you break it down into enough small steps.

—Henry Ford

When asked about his plans for retirement, Muhammad Ali gave one of his trademark illustrative explanations on the concept of time and just how little of it we really have. "Of the next thirty years," he said, "I'll be asleep nine of those years, I have to travel for four years, and about three years will be spent on entertainment [TV, movies, etc.]. When it's all said and done, I might have about fourteen years to be productive!"

The champ's immaculate way with words drove home an amazing point: our time is and will always be the most valuable thing we own. How we spend it is up to no one but us.

145

Successful people in all walks of life tend to be time-management gurus. If you want to be extremely successful in college—or in life—you'll most likely spend some time each day grappling with how to get the most quality work done in the least amount of time. Filled with distractions and opportunities, your undergraduate years demand that you become a masterful time manager. How you decide to manage your time will affect every aspect of your undergraduate career. For instance, learning how to network is rather pointless if you never have the time to do any networking.

This chapter provides ten time-management hacks for your success. Read and reread this chapter when your semester gets overwhelming and you fall into bad habits. Soak up the concepts until you know all ten like the back of your hand. Sometimes just a reminder that time is your most valuable asset will spur you to implement one or two of these practices and regain control of life's most valuable resource.

1) Don't Begin Your Day Until It Is Complete

Takeaway: Write down your daily goals on a physical piece of paper every day.

Author and business philosopher Jim Rohn said it best: "Never begin the day until it is finished on paper." We all know the impact of using a calendar and a schedule. If you make a commitment to becoming the architect of your day—and then actually convert it to a habit—you will have unparalleled results. Now, you might be thinking, "Isaac, I get it. But I don't need to write out my days. I have it all up here [index finger points to temple]."

Putting too much trust in your memory is the easiest way to fall into the habit of mismanaging your activities. Additionally, studies on psychomotor learning have shown that the physical act of writing down your objectives has a great positive impact on your ability to meet those objectives. You'll stick to a plan much more consistently when it's in your pocket on a physical piece of paper and not just on your smartphone or in your memory. Each night, write out your next day in its entirety. Then watch it unfold.

2) Set SMART Goals

Takeaway: Use SMART goal setting to keep you on track and aligned with your short- and long-term goals.

Goal setting can be tricky at times. We experience a great sense of satisfaction when we achieve something we set out to do. However, just the idea of falling short of a goal deters many of us from ever setting clear, well-defined goals for ourselves.

SMART goals help us to alleviate this issue. The acronym SMART stands for specific, measurable, actionable, realistic, and time-bound. By using this acronym to set our goals, we give ourselves a better chance to not only hit our aimed target but also decide on the target that is right for us to begin with.

Let's use the example of wanting to grow our network to see how the SMART method can help us achieve this goal.

Specific

"I want to grow my network vs. I want to gain five new contacts in the tech industry."

Taking the time to define your goal with specific language helps you understand clearly what it is you are looking for. *I want to grow my network* is a vague goal that can be achieved in a variety of ways. Because of this, it may be difficult to identify what immediate steps you need to take to go about achieving this goal. *I want to gain five new contacts in the tech industry* is a goal that is specific and painstakingly clear, giving you the information you need to take immediate action.

Measurable

When we are setting a goal, it is imperative that we pose the following question: *By what measure will I know when my goal is 25 percent, 50 percent, 75 percent or 100 percent complete?* By setting a goal that is measurable, we can hold ourselves accountable throughout the entire process. Without being able to track our progress, it is easy to lose motivation for accomplishing that goal. The more chances we give ourselves to pat ourselves on the back with measurable checkpoints, the greater the chance that we continue to follow through and reach the completion of our goal.

Actionable

What are the definite action steps I can take to achieve this goal? For example, in order to gain five new tech industry contacts as a part of your network, you can 1) attend a tech conference or 2) use the alumni database to email alumni working in the tech industry. These are definite action steps that help you move towards the completion of this goal.

It is not uncommon that people grow stagnant because they fail to identify actionable steps before creating the goal. Make sure you identify the one or two action steps that help you move towards the completion of your goal.

Realistic

Is this goal realistic for me? Usually, this is a question that you can revisit after you've taken your definite action steps. You set a goal for gaining five new contacts in the tech industry, but after a month of consistent emailing you are finding it difficult to get even one individual on the phone. In this case, finding five new contacts may be unrealistic for you and too much of a demand on your schedule, and that's perfectly fine. Reset your goal and aim for a more realistic number moving forward.

Time-bound

Deadlines help us perform. When we set a goal that is time-bound, it helps to prioritize our time accordingly. In order to gain five new contacts, we need to know how much time we should dedicate towards: attending off-campus conferences, writing networking emails, setting aside time for phone calls, etc. As you can see, there are sub-goals within goals. The more work you put into creating deadlines for each of these steps, the easier the attaining of the goal will be.

3) Follow the 80/20 Rule

Takeaway: Focus on the activities that matter most.

The 80/20 Rule, also known as the Pareto Principle, is a well-established time management rule of thumb stating that 20 percent of our activities are worth 80 percent of our results. Your time in college illustrates the Pareto Principle in motion. Have you ever had one of those days where you were busy the entire day yet accomplished very little? We all have these days, when we direct attention to the easy activities that don't help us all that much and ignore the one or two tasks that, if completed that day, would really move the needle forward in our lives. For instance, you might reorganize your class notes, search out a favorite study spot, and finish writing a post for a class, but neglect to start that massive term paper you've been dreading. Or you might go online and browse job openings for hours but fail to send one e-mail to a potential employer. These are examples of pushing away the most important tasks and welcoming the menial tasks—the 80 percent that has very little effect on your overall progress toward your goals.

The 80/20 rule is simple to understand yet revolutionary in its effect. To implement it, first identify what is most important in your day, your week, or your semester. Focus on the tasks that will give you the best return on your time. Just one week of applying the 80/20 rule will make you more productive than you've ever been. Try it out, and watch your results multiply.

4) Learn to Say No

Takeaway: It's okay to say no to other people's requests. Learn to grow comfortable with making yourself the priority.

College is filled with all kinds of alluring distractions, and saying no to them isn't easy. In fact, saying no can be the most difficult challenge college students face. For example, your best friend invites you to attend the big game at the last minute. Everyone's going to be at the dance performance tomorrow night. You're dying to check out a free movie, a concert, an alumni brunch, and the premier of your favorite TV show—and all these events are happening next week. How can you say no? And if you *do* say no, what goes and what stays? The task of filtering these activities to find what deserves your attention and what doesn't is what makes college a four-year-long time-management course.

Although these decisions are incredibly difficult, you must make them in order to stay aligned with your goals— getting the grades you've committed to, building your network, staying in shape, and so on. When you begin to take control over your schedule, you will soon find out that it is impossible to please everyone and to do everything. On the positive side, you might also feel some relief to admit, finally, that you simply can't do it all.

Saying no isn't easy at first, but your self-control muscles will strengthen with practice. You'll become wiser and put yourself in situations that support your success. For example, it's very hard to be tempted by a TV if you study in a room with no TV! The people in your circle will begin to respect you, your time, and your display of control over your own schedule. Instead of expecting you to tag along to a game that starts in an hour, they'll start asking you two days in advance. Some of your friends might even begin to apply these techniques in their own lives.

Learning to say no saves you from becoming a yes-man in college. Yes-men have sent more grades down the drain than you could ever imagine:

"You should come with me to the mall!"

"Yes!"

"How about we stay up and watch reruns tonight?"

"Sure!"

"What about the game? Lunch? Party?"

"Yes! Yes! Yes!"

The yes-man syndrome can win you friends, sure, but if you're not on top of your priorities, you'll end up behind on the things that matter most—and that commonly means your grades. Once you grasp this truth, you'll understand that the phrase "No, thank you" has the power to keep you focused on achieving the best results for you.

In order to keep your relationships healthy, it's important to be both cordial and creative when turning down invitations. This allows you to say no without burning bridges. Let's take your friend's last-minute invitation to the game as an example. You can't attend because you have carved out those two hours to study for an upcoming exam. A suitable response would be as follows: "You know I would love to be there, but I'm behind on studying for my huge exam coming up. Can we hang out next week and catch up? I'll be done with my exam." With these words, you've turned down the offer with grace.

5) Practice Deep Work

Takeaway: Create the time and space to complete your most difficult, demanding tasks from start to finish.

The concept of deep work comes from Cal Newport, associate professor at Georgetown University and author of *Deep Work: Rules for Focused Success in a Distracted World*. As Newport defines it, "Deep work is the ability to focus without distraction on a cognitively demanding task. It's a skill that allows you to quickly master complicated information and produce better results in less time."

According to Newport, the purpose of time management is to produce better results in less time. In today's society, we've been sold the false idea that multitasking is effective. Don't fall for this trap! Multitasking is effective in its efforts to make us *feel* productive, but not actually *be* productive. As our cognitive awareness shifts from reading the article to writing the paper to watching the game, we perpetuate the illusion that we are accomplishing more when in fact we are accomplishing less while producing lower-quality work.

Engaging in deep work means producing your best work when you need it. To do so, follow these simple steps.

1) At the start of your week, sit down and decide on the single task that will have the greatest impact on you. What task do you absolutely need to get done but have been dodging for some time? What task takes a high level of concentration to get done the right way?

2) After identifying this one task, carve out a block of time that week—preferably a thirty-, sixty-, or ninety-minute period—for uninterrupted work.

3) When the time arrives, make sure you're in a distraction-free environment. Make sure your work area is completely void of anything that could cause even the slightest of distraction—a ringing or vibrating phone, notifications that pop up on your computer screen, a roommate playing loud music, and so on.

4) Get to work! If necessary, set a timer and see to it that you work singularly on the task at hand for the allotted time.

Working in this way—deeply—just once or twice a week can help you achieve some amazing results.

6) Limit Social Media: Attention Residue

Takeaway: Create a block of time to visit social media sites.

Social media in itself isn't a bad thing, but the ways in which we use it can become detrimental to our productivity. Cal Newport uses the term "attention residue" to refer to the mental processes that continue to occur after we move from one activity to the next. This residue gradually builds when we hop on and off Facebook, Instagram, and the various social media outlets we visit throughout the day.

154

Outside of our awareness, this stop-and-start effect inhibits our ability to focus on other tasks and wears on us over the course of a day.

Instead of checking your social-media pages multiple times throughout the day, consider selecting specific blocks of time to visit quick-hit social media sites like Facebook and Instagram. For example, after your last class of the day, take thirty minutes to catch up with your friends' posts. This strategy provides more structure within your day and leads to better online habits. It also minimizes the number of occasions when the social-media world consumes you. You probably know what I'm talking about—when you get so lost in the Facebook, Instagram, or YouTube that you miss an entire meal, or you look away from your computer and forget where exactly you are. We've all been there. The better you can control the social-media craze, the better off your brain will be—and the more effectively you will reach your goals.

7) The Power of Weekly Reviews

Takeaway: Set a hard date and time for weekly reviews of your production.

Sit down at the beginning of your semester. On your calendar (make sure you have a calendar that is physically visible in your dorm room as well as on your electronic devices), set a reminder for a specific day and time every week. Title this thirty-minute window "Weekly Review." During these thirty minutes, separate your tasks into categories (academic, athletic, social, and so on) and answer the following questions:

- What three major tasks did I accomplish this week?

- What's one thing I want to improve upon?

- What was the most productive day of the week for me? Why?

Note that two of these questions are designed so that your answers will be positive. This weekly review is not only a mental boost for you—we all need a mental pick-me-up sometimes—but also a weekly reset button. When you reach the thick of the semester, you will be thankful when these days come around! It's always good to take note of the great work you are doing and to plan your "reset." As the saying goes, we can only improve the things that we measure. If you find that Thursdays are consistently great days for getting work done, plan to do your most important work on Thursday in the upcoming week. In other words, use what you learn from these weekly reviews to improve on your schedule week by week. Use this technique to your advantage, and watch as the benefits pile up throughout the academic year.

8) The Power of Reverse Engineering

Takeaway: Find someone who is achieving the results you want, and duplicate their efforts.

It was said that in the Syrian war with the Egyptians, the Assyrian soldiers were successful in large part due to their chariots. The chariots were effective war vehicles well ahead of their time and left their enemies in awe. In a sequence of events, the Egyptians captured one chariot, studied it, and reverse engineered it into what we now know as the Egyptian chariot. The Egyptian chariot was a great improvement over the original Syrian chariot, but had it not been for the Egyptians' ability to study and re-create this marvel of technology, the new chariot never would have existed.

Reverse engineering, by definition, is the process of extracting knowledge or design features from something and reproducing it based on that knowledge. You can apply the process of reverse engineering to your study habits. You can save yourself an incredible amount of time and effort by studying and copying the habits of people who are getting the results you desire.

This strategy takes a dose of courage and two doses of humility. Keep reminding yourself that asking for help or advice is a sign of maturity, not weakness. Some people allow themselves to remain stuck as C students because they fear rejection. Take pride in asking for help. Take pride in being someone who does what is necessary to save time and to get ahead in life.

9) Eat That Frog!

Takeaway: Develop the habit of tackling your most difficult task first.

Procrastination and college go hand in hand. One way to combat the tendency to put things off is to do the most difficult, most important tasks first. Every day, ask yourself, "What is the single most difficult, arduous, time-consuming task that awaits me today?" This task is usually the very one you put off over and over, until it's the last item left on your to-do list. After spending most of your cognitive energy on comparatively meaningless tasks throughout the day, it's no wonder when you fall short on completing your most important task.

So, how do you combat this kind of backward thinking? First, you have to make a vow to get straight to it. You have to do the task now, because sometimes later becomes never.

As author Brian Tracy says, "If you eat the frog first, it ain't pretty. But you know that it will be the most difficult thing you do all day." Don't stop until you've eaten the complete frog. Know that even if this task is the only thing you do, it'll be worth all the rest combined. Practicing this habit, even only a few times a week, will increase your productivity and leave you feeling more energized than when you began.

10) Plan Your Fun and Incentivize!

Takeaway: Let your fun be the reward for your work.

One of the reasons many dread spending energy on time management is that they only plan the work aspects of their lives! We create schedules for classes and study sessions; we know when we should go to sleep and when we should wake up. But why don't we schedule our leisure activities? We certainly can. In fact, creating schedules for upcoming social events and weekend plans can make you more productive if you use them in the right way.

Try this, for example. If you want to attend a concert at the end of the week, sit down and plan out what the week will need to look like for you to enjoy the concert without guilt. What tasks should you complete? How many assignments? How many job applications? When you plan your fun, you give yourself a bonus chance to plan your work.

Don't be afraid to tie your work and your fun together. Get in the habit of creating work-fun schedules, where one can't be done without the other. As you may have suspected, it works both ways. If you plan your work and complete the objective, be sure to celebrate! College is about balance. Plan your fun, and allow this strategy to help you achieve your goals.

Chapter Takeaways

- Time is your most valuable asset. If you don't manage your time in college properly, there's no way you will be able to network. Use one, some, or all of the time-saving strategies in this chapter to help you win back your time and get more done on a day-to-day basis.

Calls to Action

- Identify your three SMART (specific, measurable, attainable, realistic, timely) goals for the academic year. Write them down on a 3 x 5 card, and laminate it. Place your goals in a visible and accessible place (dorm room wall, wallet, purse, etc.).

- Every night for one week, sit down and write out your goals for the next day. This will be difficult the first time. Stick with it.

- Create an accountability group for your long-term goals. Ask friends, roommates, or family members to help check on your progress.

CONCLUSION

You have come to the end of *How to Network in College*. For the past ten chapters, you have received a step-by-step formula, a game plan, and a practical guide all wrapped into one. This book will help you cultivate some amazing relationships during your time in college. But even more important than the people you meet is the maturation process you will encounter along the way. After all, these networking strategies are meant to aid in both your personal and professional development. Ralph Waldo Emerson captured the essence of networking as well as the central theme of the entire book in one sentence: *"Every man I meet is in some way my superior; and in that I can learn from him."*

In an ideal world, you will take the first of a series of steps towards your success *today*. Take the time to internalize what networking is and how it can help you as you review chapter one. Invest the time necessary to uncover your strengths, passions, interests, and weaknesses—let these critical answers serve as your compass when searching for internships and job opportunities in the near future.

Build your personal brand. Create a standout LinkedIn profile, order your networking business cards, and begin your personal blog to help bolster and amplify your online presence. When the time comes for you to reach out to strangers and attempt to make them your allies, revisit chapter four to ensure that your email etiquette is grounded in its fundamentals. Use the e-mail templates provided to contact professionals in the industry who can help you land that interview, secure that job offer, or maybe even begin that new startup you've always dreamed about.

Remember that there is an art to networking when in one-on-one situations. Use chapter five to sharpen your communicative skills so that you can ace your coffee talk with the potential boss, or impress the interviewee over the phone with your well-researched questions about a company's history. Utilize the *five ingredients of a great first impression* to connect with anyone, anywhere, at anytime.

Should you fall short on motivation, come back to chapter six to remind yourself of the power of *thinking big*. Shoot for the stars—you have nothing to lose and virtually everything to gain when you decide to try and network with individuals who could change the trajectory of your career. Remember, networking always presents a win-win scenario. You either win or you learn. Use the Tim Ferriss story for inspiration to help you *think big* and swing for the fences every now and again.

And we cannot forget what we've learned from Professor Granovetter: when it comes to discovering new opportunities of any kind, weak tie relationships are in fact more beneficial than our strong ties. Therefore, make new friends on campus and create a schedule that allows you to see more of your college and interact with those whom you otherwise would never get a chance to meet. Many college students can go four years and meet only a handful of their classmates out of the thousands that cross their paths. Don't let this be you.

Building your network off campus is just as important as building your network on campus. Be sure to volunteer at least once a year for a big-city conference. Dress well, do more than what is expected, and always be ready to deliver your PEP Talk at the drop of a dime. Remember also to stay in touch with your high school alumni groups to keep your network both well balanced and well rooted.

And don't forget your mentors! If you need help, ask for help from the right people as discussed in chapter nine. Ask people who have accomplished something you wish to accomplish in the most direct manner, "How did you do it?" Let go of your ego and let others help you get to where you want to go. Also, remember that you have gifts, talents, and experiences that no one else has. Take the time to identify these talents and become a mentor. Return the favor and give back. Experience the profound awesomeness of helping others become better versions of themselves. There's not a more rewarding feeling in the world.

I wish nothing but success for you and your time in college. If you take away only one idea, let it be the following: Networking is the key to your future success.

Cultivate the right relationships, land the perfect job, and create the kinds of experiences that will make college the best time of your life.

Happy Networking!

Isaac

www.isaacserwanga.com

ABOUT THE AUTHOR

Isaac Serwanga is an educational consultant, speaker, and an advocate for the personal and professional development of high school and college students. He graduated from Princeton University with a degree in Sociology in 2013, where he also excelled as a football, basketball, and track and field Division-I student-athlete. Isaac is the co-creator of Profound Ivy, a career mentoring program for college student athletes which has served as the springboard for *How to Network in College*. Through his work, Isaac's primary mission is to provide the younger generation with the information and inspiration necessary to fulfill their highest potential.

Made in the USA
Coppell, TX
12 June 2020